A Kid's Guide
TO THE
Smithsonian

SMITHSONIAN
INSTITUTION
PRESS

WASHINGTON
DC

ILLUSTRATIONS
BY STEVEN
ROTBLATT

EDITED BY
BARBARA
EMBURY
HEHNER

A KID'S GUIDE
TO THE
SMITHSONIAN

BY ANN PHILLIPS BAY

WELCOME

CONTENTS

◆ Names in parentheses are shortened versions of the actual exhibit or hall names as you will find them in each museum. These names also appear on the floorplan maps and near the page number at the bottom of most pages.

NATIONAL MUSEUM OF AMERICAN HISTORY

NATIONAL AIR AND SPACE MUSEUM

LAST BUT NOT LEAST

The oldest Smithsonian "museum" is the red sandstone building affectionately known as the Castle. Designed by James Renwick, Jr., the original Smithsonian building now houses the Smithsonian Information Center. Near the Mall entrance to the Castle, a crypt holds the remains of James Smithson, the British scientist whose gift of money to the United States led to the founding of the Smithsonian a century and a half ago.

The National Air and Space Museum, which opened on America's Bicentennial, July 4, 1976, shows you the whole history of flight. Unlike the other museums in this book, almost everything at Air and Space dates from the twentieth century. In fact, some exhibits invite you to imagine how we'll explore space in the twenty-first century.

The building that houses the National Museum of American History is a relative newcomer that opened in 1964. But some of its collections date back to the earliest days of the Smithsonian: in 1858 the Institution received all the treasures from the National Cabinet of Curiosities, which had been founded in 1790. The collecting at American History never stops, and will continue as long as there are new events, inventions, fashions, and hobbies to document.

The National Museum of Natural History, which opened in 1910, is the largest research museum in the United States. Of the over 140 million things at the Smithsonian, 118 million are in the collections of the Natural History Museum! Here you'll be able to see—and sometimes touch—some of the oldest, biggest, and most amazing things in the universe.

You call this a Mall? Where are all the stores?

You birdbrain! The National Mall is a long, grassy esplanade stretching from the Capitol to the Washington Monument.

Meteorites. Dinosaurs. Egyptian mummies. Locomotives. Tarantulas and diamonds. Microchips and spaceships. George Washington's false teeth and Oscar the Grouch's trash can. Two hundred and eighty-two aircraft, 300,000 water bugs, 12 million postage stamps, and 20 million seashells. In all, the Smithsonian Institution has about 140 million things in its collection. If you only looked at each thing for a minute, it would take you about 266 years (with no time for sleeping!) to look at them all. Fortunately, only about two million of these objects are on display at any one time. And millions of visitors come to Washington every year to see them.

The Smithsonian Institution is a collection of sixteen museums and art galleries—as well as the National Zoo. All but two of the museums are in Washington (these two are in New York City), and nine of the Washington museums are on the National Mall between the U.S. Capitol and the Washington Monument.

Big as the Smithsonian museums and galleries are, the part you can see is just a tiny fraction of the whole Institution. The Smithsonian has an observatory in Arizona and a research institute in Panama working to save the rainforest, as well as many other research centers. Hundreds of scientists work at the Smithsonian—120 of them at the National Museum of Natural History alone—and they travel all over the world gathering knowledge. Smithsonian experts also share their knowledge with other researchers, doing everything from identifying rare insects to figuring out the age of a fragile piece of lace to helping the FBI solve murders.

Over 6,500 people work for the Smithsonian Institution. The

OME TO THE SMITHSONIAN

range of things they do is just as astounding as the collections themselves. Some of them are involved in acquiring new items for the Smithsonian, and in carefully cataloging them when they arrive. Curators decide how the items should be displayed—should they be part of an exhibit that is already in one of the museums, or should a new exhibit be planned? Conservators clean objects and figure out how they can be preserved from dust, sun-

light, and other things that could harm them. Designers plan and create exciting museum displays. People in education departments plan talks, guided tours, and other programs for children and adults. And a large group of museum guards, security staff, and volunteer tour leaders (called "docents") help make sure visitors get where they're going and find what they're looking for.

If you're able to visit in person, the Information Center in

the Smithsonian Castle has brochures, maps, models, videos, and interactive "touch screens"—as well as friendly people—to help you plan what to see. Next door to the Castle is the Arts and Industries Building. It's the second-oldest Smithsonian building on the Mall, completed in 1871. It was built to house all the treasures from the 1876 Philadelphia Centennial Exposition (finally the Castle was just too small!) and it

still contains objects from that exhibit. You can see what kinds of things amazed people in the nineteenth century—and how these things used to be displayed. What a change there's been since then, as you're about to find out. From the dawn of time to a vision of the future, you can discover it all at the Smithsonian!

A REVOLUTIONARY IDEA

Above: In this 1863 photo of Independence Avenue, the Smithsonian Castle Building stands alone on the Mall.

Left: Joseph Henry, first Secretary (or head) of the Smithsonian, relaxes with his wife Harriet and their daughters.

Museums are so much a part of our lives that it may be a surprise to find out they didn't exist through most of human history. Kings or other wealthy people often had collections of paintings or sculptures, or exotic plants and animals brought back by explorers. But ordinary people never got a chance to see these wonders. This began to change in the eighteenth century. It was an age of revolution in Europe—and also in America. It was a time when many people began to believe that everyone had the right to be educated and to have a voice in the government of their country. Being able to visit museums was seen as an important part of this education. Soon public museums were being established to meet the new demand. The British Museum in London and the Louvre in Paris—still important museums today—opened in the late 1700s.

The United States only had a handful of museums—the first was in Charleston, South Carolina—before 1800. By 1876, however, it had over two hundred. In that year, the Smithsonian was already thirty years old, yet it was still all housed in one building—the red sandstone structure that everyone at the Smithsonian calls the Castle. The Castle somehow contained a science museum, a lecture hall, an art gallery, research labs, and offices—with room left over to be the home of the Smithsonian's Secretary and his family!

THANKS, MR. SMITHSON!

The Smithsonian Institution began with a gift of money from a man who never even set foot in the United States. His name was James Smithson, and he was an English scientist. When he died in 1829, he left his huge fortune to his nephew. However, Smithson's will stated that if the nephew died childless—which he did in 1835—the fortune would be given to the United States. The money was to be used "to found, at Washington, under the name of the Smithsonian Institution, an establishment for the increase and diffusion of knowledge." It took a few years for the United States government to decide how the money should be used. In 1846, President James Polk finally signed into law an act establishing the Smithsonian Institution.

Smithson never explained why he was leaving his money to the United States instead of his own country. He had been the victim of snobbery in England, which may have had something to do with it. He also wished his name to become famous—and he may have felt that an institution named after him had a better chance of standing out in a young country. Europe already had many famous collections of treasures by the early nineteenth century. The United States did not—but all that was about to change.

WHOOOO'S THERE?

In addition to people who once made their home in the Smithsonian Castle building, the towering structure also has a history of some *feathered* residents.

A Smithsonian Secretary named S. Dillon Ripley, fascinated by stories he heard of owls that had once lived in the towers of the Castle, set out in 1971 to bring them back. The first owl family placed there didn't remain long, so a second group was introduced in 1977. These barn owls were first trained at the National Zoo. Staff members took turns climbing five sets of ladders into the Castle's west tower to leave dead rats for the owls. They also kept a log of the birds' behavior. The owls were named "Increase" and "Diffusion," after the part of James Smithson's will that described the Smithsonian's mission as the "increase and diffusion of knowledge."

Sadly, the second owl pair soon flew the roost as well. But to this day the birds are thought of as unofficial Smithsonian mascots.

PLANNING A VISIT?

Not everyone can visit the Smithsonian in person, but each year some ten million people do! If you happen to be planning a trip to the world's largest museum complex, we've included a few features that can help make your visit a lot easier—and a lot more fun.

You probably know there's no easy answer to the question "where's the Smithsonian?" That's because there is no *one* place to go. In fact, once you arrive in Washington, D.C., the Smithsonian is all over—with nine museums on the National Mall alone. It's enough to tire you out just thinking about it, but these two pages will help you get your bearings fast. With this book, you'll be able to figure out exactly what you want to see—and learn a little about it—before you even leave home. Once you're here, you can use this book to help you get around; to make sure you don't miss any of the coolest stuff; and to find out some inside tips for making the most of your visit. You'll even go behind the scenes and discover some things no visitor can *ever* see.

To take you on a tour of each and every Smithsonian museum, this book would have to be ten times the size it is—and you'd never get it into your backpack. So, we've made things a little more manageable by zooming in on three museums kids especially love to spend time in. This book is your guide to a selection of star attractions at the three big Smithsonian Mall museums—the National Museum of Natural History, the National Museum of American History, and the National Air and Space Museum. (There's also a short guide to the other Smithsonian museums and galleries and their treasures on pages 148-153.) We only feature highlights, so think of this guide as a starting point for planning a visit suited to your own interests and imagination.

You'll soon see that it's not hard to find your way to the wonders of the Smithsonian—you just have to know where to look.

CRACKING THE COLOR CODE

Each of the three featured museums in this book have been color-coded, so you'll always know exactly where you are. The color strip along the right-hand edge of the book is different for each museum section—red for Natural History, green for American History, and blue for Air and Space.

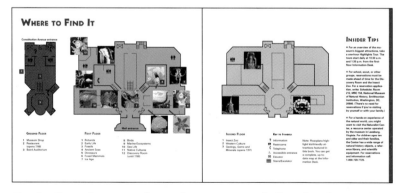

On the floorplan maps for each museum, each floor has been color-coded too. Within museum sections, page numbers and exhibit names at the bottom of the page are keyed to floorplan map colors so you'll always know what floor you're on.

Is It Real ◆ ◆ ◆ or Rotblatt?

As you look through this book, you'll find a number of illustrations that at first seem to fool your eyes. They don't exactly look like photographs, but they don't entirely look like drawings either. That's because they're *both!* We gave an illustrator named Steven Rotblatt some photographs of actual Smithsonian exhibits, and invited him to turn them into fanciful creations from his own imagination. As a result, some parts of the photographs still look like the exhibit, while other parts definitely do not. Above are our "before" and "after" looks at the Life in the Ancient Seas exhibit in the Natural History Museum.

If you happen to be making a visit to the Smithsonian, you can have fun finding which exhibits inspired the whimsical drawings in this book.

Survival Tips

◆ The Smithsonian is the largest museum complex in the world, so you'll be doing *lots* of walking. The Air and Space Museum, all by itself, is three city blocks long. The National Mall, where you'll find nine of the Smithsonian museums, is about ten city blocks long. Wear your most comfortable clothes and shoes.

◆ When is the best time to visit the Smithsonian? If you want to avoid the crowds, come in the wintertime. If you're visiting in the summer, try to get to museums as soon as they open in the morning. Museums are less crowded on weekdays than on weekends.

◆ Every museum has an information desk. Make it your first stop. The staff has brochures to help you plan your visit. They can also tell you about exhibits and special events that kids enjoy.

◆ There's lots to see at the Smithsonian—but there's also lots to do. If you start to get tired of just looking at things, find a "hands on" room or exhibit—many of the museums have one.

◆ Take a break from time to time. Eat a snack or a meal in one of the museum restaurants, or have a picnic with your family on the National Mall. You can toss a frisbee, fly a kite, or take a ride on the antique carousel.

◆ Plan your visit ahead of time. You can get a "family package" of information by calling (202) 357-2700. Then you—and the other people in your family—can figure out which things you especially want to see and find out where they are. It makes more sense to see a few things that really interest you than to tire yourself out trying to see too much.

NATIONAL MUSEUM OF NATURAL HISTORY

WELCOME TO A WORLD OF WONDERS

NATIONAL MUSEUM OF NATURAL HISTORY
CONSTITUTION AVENUE AT 10TH STREET, NW
MALL ENTRANCE (SHOWN LEFT):
MADISON DRIVE BETWEEN 9TH AND 12TH STREETS, NW

If you've ever strolled along a beach, or beside a pond, or through the woods, enjoying the things you see, then you know how much fun a nature walk can be. Exploring the National Museum of Natural History is a lot like taking a nature walk—but in some ways even better. Here, under one big roof, is a whole world of nature and human life for you to discover, from the tiniest insects of today to the largest dinosaurs of 100 million years ago, from the native peoples of Asia to the native peoples of North America. You can visit the mountains of South America, the plains of Africa, and the bottom of a 500-million-year-old sea—and still be back in time for lunch!

If you enter the museum from the Mall, you'll find yourself in a big round room with a ceiling that goes all the way up to the roof, four stories up. This room is called the *rotunda*. Off the rotunda, on the museum's first and second floors, are the major exhibit halls. The entrance to each hall is marked by a banner telling you what you can find there. On the next two pages we show you some of the highlights kids most like to explore.

Decide where you want to begin—and start a journey across thousands of miles and billions of years.

WHERE TO FIND IT

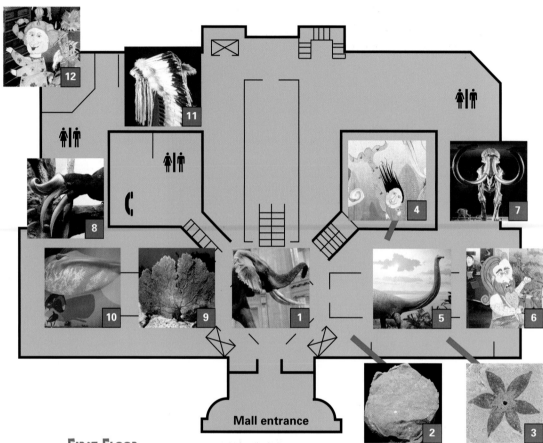

Constitution Avenue entrance

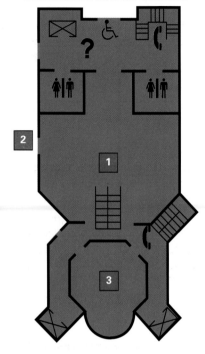

GROUND FLOOR

1 Museum Shop
2 Restaurant
  (opens 7/98)
3 Baird Auditorium

FIRST FLOOR

1 Rotunda
2 Early Life
3 Fossils
4 Ancient Seas
5 Dinosaurs
6 Fossil Mammals
7 Ice Age

8 Birds
9 Marine Ecosystems
10 Sea Life
11 Native Cultures
12 Discovery Room
   (until 7/98)

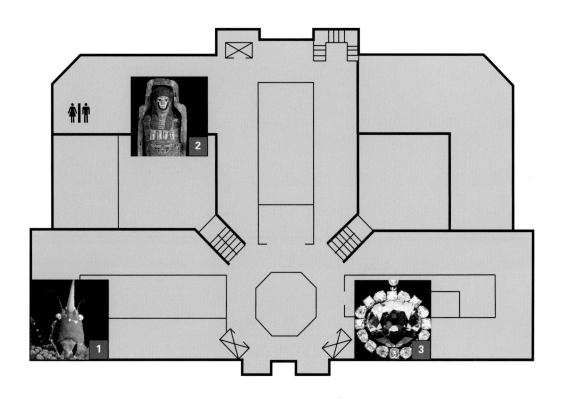

Second Floor

1 Insect Zoo
2 Western Culture
3 Geology, Gems and
   Minerals (opens 7/97)

Key to Symbols

? Information
👫 Restrooms
📞 Telephone
♿ Accessible entrance
⊠ Elevator
▦ Stairs/Escalator

Note: Floorplans high-
light kid-friendly at-
tractions featured in
this book. You can get
a complete, up-to-
date map at the Infor-
mation Desk.

Insider Tips

◆ For an overview of the museum's biggest attractions, take
a one-hour Highlights Tour. The
tours start daily at 10:30 a.m.
and 1:30 p.m. from the first-
floor Information Desk.

◆ For school, scout, or other
groups, reservations must be
made ahead of time for the Discovery Room and the Insect
Zoo. For a reservation applica-
tion, write: Scheduler, Room
212, MRC 158, National Museum
of Natural History, Smithsonian
Institution, Washington, DC,
20560. (There's no need for
reservations if you're visiting
by yourself or with your family.)

◆ For a hands-on experience of
the natural world, you might
want to visit the Naturalist Center, a resource center operated
by the museum in Leesburg,
Virginia. For children ages ten
and older and their families,
the Center has a wide range of
natural history objects, a reference library, and scientific
equipment. For reservations
and information call:
1-800-729-7725.

THE ROTUNDA ELEPHANT

Ever since the late 1950s, the elephant in the rotunda has greeted visitors to the museum. With his tail and trunk held high, he has an adventuresome look about him, as if he's about to take a run or a stroll on the grassy African plain—called a *savannah*—which was his home.

He is unusually big, even for an African elephant. When alive, he weighed a full 12 tons, which is about 5 tons more than the average adult elephant.

In 1955, a hunter killed him and had his skin shipped to the Smithsonian. Museum workers mounted the skin on a wooden frame, which they had built in the elephant's shape. When the giant specimen was finally finished, they placed it in the center of the rotunda for visitors to see. The museum estimates that every year more than 6 million people stop to have a look at him.

An elephant's big, strong ivory tusks help it to get food and water. With its tusks, it can plow up the ground to find roots to eat, or pry open tree trunks to reach the soft wood inside. It can also drill into the ground to find water. In addition, male elephants sometimes use their tusks as weapons when fighting rivals over female elephants. In case you're wondering whether both male and female elephants have tusks, the answer is: both yes and no! Among African elephants, both males and females have tusks, but among Asian elephants, only the males have them.

What can an elephant do with its trunk?

With its 50,000 muscles, an elephant's trunk is an amazing multi-purpose tool. Just imagine our elephant using its trunk *as a hose,* for spraying itself with water and dousing itself with dust; *as a nose,* for smelling; *as an arm,* for reaching high into the tree-tops to gather leaves to eat; *as a trumpet,* for calling other elephants; and *as a hand,* for picking things up and carrying them, as well as for greeting other elephants with a friendly "trunk shake."

THE MAGNIFICENT VOYAGE

Everyone knows about the voyages of Columbus, Magellan, and Captain Cook. But few people have heard of Lt. Charles Wilkes. Yet his amazing voyages of discovery brought back to the United States thousands of priceless objects that became the starting point for the National Museum of Natural History's vast collections. It all began in 1838, when naval lieutenant Wilkes commanded one of the most important scientific and technological expeditions ever made—the U.S. Exploring Expedition. With six ships, he made a four-year, 139,000-kilometer (87,000-mile) voyage around the world. The expedition was filled with storms, shipwrecks, battles—and important discoveries. Wilkes charted, for the first time, large parts of the Pacific Ocean, including the Hawaiian and Fiji Islands, and explored Australia. He braved icy, storm-tossed seas to map 2400 kilometers (1500 miles) of the Antarctic Coast, at a time when many doubted that a South Pole continent even existed. The scientists aboard the ships collected thousands of fossils, gemstones, plants, corals, seashells, butterflies, and other creatures that were new to science. They also collected thousands of masks, weapons, clothing, and other items from the native peoples of the Pacific Islands and the North American West Coast. A few years after Wilkes returned, these treasures were turned over to the newly founded Smithsonian. And what about Wilkes himself? Although his name is forgotten, he inspired one of the most famous characters in American literature—Captain Ahab in Herman Melville's *Moby Dick!*

DIGGING INTO THE PAST

ERA	PERIOD		MILLIONS OF YEARS AGO
CENOZOIC	Quaternary		
			1.6
	Tertiary		
			66.4
MESOZOIC	Cretaceous		
			144
	Jurassic		
			208
	Triassic		
			245
PALEOZOIC		Permian	
			286
	Carboniferous	Pennsylvanian	
			320
		Mississippian	
			360
	Devonian		
			408
	Silurian		
			438
	Ordovician		
			505
	Cambrian		
			570
PRECAMBRIAN			

One of the most exciting stories told in this museum is about *change*. It's the story of how the earth was born and life began. Starting with one-celled organisms, life slowly, over millions of years, became more varied and more complex. While this was happening, the earth itself changed: seas appeared and dried up, continents formed, slammed into each other, and broke apart, and the climate changed from tropical to icy and back again. Gradually the plants and animals we know today—from ants to elephants, from oak trees to buttercups, and people, too—came into being. To piece together this story of never-ending change, scientists turn to fossil evidence much as a detective uses clues to solve a mystery.

HOW OLD IS OLD ?

What does it mean to say that something is old? You might call a photograph of your grandmother, taken when she was young, an "old" picture. Maybe your family has some antique furniture dating from 100 or 200 years ago. But to paleontologists, who study the evidence of ancient fossils, none of the things in your home is old. Even the oldest things in human history, like the pyramids, aren't truly old to them. Paleontologists don't think in terms of hundreds of years, or even thousands, but millions and millions of years.

Human history began about 10,000 years ago, when people first began to farm and form settled communities. About 5,000 years ago, people invented writing. From written records we get much of our information about the *historic* past.

Everything that happened before that occurred in the *prehistoric* past, that is, "the time before history." It stretches all the way back from about 10,000 years ago to the earth's very beginnings, about 4.6 *billion* years ago. But how do we keep track of such an immense amount of time?

Scientists have divided time into three huge chunks called *eras*: the Paleozoic, Mesozoic, and Cenozoic. Each era is further divided into smaller time periods. Compared with these vast periods of time, all human history has passed in the blink of an eye!

SPACE INVADERS

Every day, invaders from space arrive in Earth's atmosphere. The invaders are meteorites—fragments of rock and metal—that come hurtling down through the atmosphere at speeds up to 70 kilometers (44 miles) per second. Most burn up before reaching Earth's surface. Of the ones that make it to the ground, most are as tiny as dust particles or grains of sand. Only a tiny proportion are bigger, and the fall of a meteor big enough to make a dent in the earth is a rare event. About 50,000 years ago, a meteorite weighing several hundred thousand tons struck northern Arizona, gouging out a crater almost a mile across.

Near the entrance to the Origins of Life exhibit, you can see the 4.6-billion-year-old Murchison meteorite, which landed in Murchison, Australia, in 1969.

To see more meteorites, including fragments of the one that landed in Arizona, look in the new Hall of Geology, Gems and Minerals on the second floor of the museum.

Above left: The Murchison meteorite is as old as the earth, and may yield clues about the birth of our solar system. It contains amino acids, the building blocks of all life.
Left: The Barringer Meteorite Crater of Arizona gouged out a hole 550 feet deep and 2.4 miles in circumference.

WHY ALL THE FUSS ABOUT FOSSILS?

Because fossils are such important evidence for scientists to use in studying the history of life on Earth, this museum has collected thousands and thousands of them. You can see, for instance, trilobites (ancient relatives of crabs and lobsters), dinosaurs of several different kinds (and their footprints!), ferns and tree trunks from long-ago swamps, a giant bird's egg, and parts of some of the earliest-known human beings.

What are fossils and why are they so special? A fossil is any evidence of life from the geologic past. It might be an actual preserved plant or animal—all of it or just part of it—or it might be just a trace the plant or animal left behind, like a leaf-print or a footprint. Billions of plants and animals have died each day, for millions of years. But most have been eaten or have rotted away to nothing, leaving no record that they were ever alive. It takes special conditions to make a fossil. Right after its death, the plant or animal must be buried so quickly that it doesn't have time to decay. Then it must be left undisturbed for thousands of years.

Top: Even the fine bristles on which this ancient worm moved are preserved in the Burgess Shale of Canada.
Middle: This squiggly worm is one of the rarest Burgess Shale fossils—only two species are known.
Bottom: A 50-million-year-old fossil flower from the shales of Colorado's Green River Formation.

During that time, chemical changes may occur to help preserve the dead plant or animal, or just a part of it. Although these changes may occur in a number of different ways, often they involve water seeping into an organism's pores and cavities. When the water evaporates, minerals that have been dissolved in it are left behind. When the minerals harden, a fossil is saved for the ages!

The hard parts of once-living things—such as bones, shells, teeth, or wood—are much more likely to become fossilized than soft parts such as leaves, fat, and skin. Can you guess why? Soft parts usually decay much faster than hard parts, before the fossilization process can get started. This means that fossils of whole plants and animals are hardly ever found. It also means that creatures that have no hard parts—worms and jellyfish, for example—are much less likely to be preserved than creatures that do.

As a fossil lies sheltered in the ground, more layers of dirt —which may contain more fossils—are deposited on top of it. As thousands and millions of years pass, the dirt may harden into layers of rock. The oldest fossils will be in the bottom layers, and the newest ones near the top.

Locked away in the ground like this, how are fossils ever found? Sometimes a river cuts a deep gorge down through the layers of rock, uncovering a fossil treasure trove for scientists to collect and study. Sometimes fossils are uncovered when rocks are cut away to make a road, a tunnel, or an excavation for a large building. What's certain is that there are far more fossils still out there than have ever been discovered. Maybe you'll be the one to make an exciting find!

This photo shows greatly enlarged one-celled micro-organisms whose fossils have been found in rocks called cherts. Scientists have been able to identify many different types of micro-organisms in these fossil deposits.

AMAZING BUT TRUE
LIFE STARTED SMALL

Some living things are so small that you can't even see them. Scientists call them *micro-organisms.* You may already know that micro-organisms are everywhere in our world today. There are trillions and trillions of them, in the air and water, on the ground, and inside you. But did you know that, in the beginning, they were the *only* forms of life? And what's more, they existed only in the oceans. For most of life's history—for about 3 billion years, in fact—there were no living things big enough to see without a microscope. (Of course, there weren't any microscopes—and nothing with eyes to look through them, either!)

The earliest micro-organisms probably had just one *cell.* Cells are the basic units of life. All organisms that you can see with your own eyes, including the tiniest insects, have many, many cells. And in case you're wondering about yourself, the estimated number of cells in a human being is, believe it or not, 75 trillion!

A scientist on a dig in Wyoming excavates fossilized dinosaur bones. The bones are encased in plaster to keep them from being damaged in transit.

wow!

DON'T MISS IT!

You can get a real "feel" for fossils at the beginning of the exhibit called A Grand Opening: Fossils Galore. Four giant rock slabs chock-full of fossils from a 440-million-year-old sea floor guard the entrance—and you can touch them!

CHARLES D. WALCOTT'S REMARKABLE FIND

One of the world's most important fossil finds came about almost by accident. In the summer of 1909, a paleontologist named Charles Doolittle Walcott was camping out with his family in the Rocky Mountains of western Canada. He tripped over a block of shale (a kind of rock formed from ancient clay or mud) and noticed the imprints of weird-looking sea creatures in the rock. Walcott had seen a lot of fossils, and he knew at once that he was looking at the whole animal—soft parts and all!

Walcott, who was also the Secretary (or head) of the Smithsonian, eventually collected 37,000 slabs of shale containing 68,000 fossils for the Institution. (Only a small sampling is on exhibit!) It took him four summers to blast and chisel them out of the rocky mountainside—and three more to collect the debris. However, it was worth every minute of the effort.

Why was the Burgess Shale site, as Walcott named it, such a wonderful discovery? Most fossils, as you've learned, record only an animal's hard parts, such as bones, shell, or teeth. A creature's soft parts—such as skin, fat and eyeballs—hardly *ever* become fossilized. But in the Burgess Shale they had somehow been preserved. Fossils of soft parts contain information that scientists can't get in any other way. They give a much better idea of what an animal looked like than hard parts alone.

The Burgess Shale fossils are also extremely old. They date back to the middle of the Cambrian period, about 530 million years ago, which makes them about twice as old as the earliest dinosaur fossils! The Burgess Shale revealed that there were more strange and varied creatures in those ancient Cambrian seas than scientists had ever imagined.

This diorama shows how some of the sea creatures preserved in the Burgess Shale looked when they were alive, 530 million years ago. The fossil lying across the diorama is *Waptia fieldensis,* an ancient crustacean.

How did the creatures in the Burgess Shale get turned into fossils?

Although we'll probably never know the answer for sure, scientists have a theory about what happened. The plants and animals of the Burgess Shale lived on a shallow mud bottom next to an underwater cliff. One day some mud poured over the top of the cliff and buried the plants and animals at the base of the cliff in deep water. It happened very quickly, sealing them off from any exposure to oxygen. Without oxygen, the buried organisms simply did not decay! Many such mud flows occurred over the years, piling up at the base of the cliff. Gradually, over thousands and thousands of years, the perfectly preserved plants and animals turned into fossils.

Left: Charles D. Walcott (with hand on hip), on the site of the Burgess Shale.

Above: As Charles Walcott worked, he kept a record, or "field notes," describing and sketching specimens and telling exactly where he had found them.

LIFE IN THE ANCIENT SEAS

Think of turtles. Think of dolphins. Think of eels and clams and whales and sharks and sand dollars. The oceans of the world are teeming with life—and have been for millions of years.

As the exhibit Life in the Ancient Seas shows us, though, countless creatures of the deep have appeared, flourished for a time, and disappeared forever. We know them only by the fossils they left behind. Some lived rooted to the ocean's bottom, looking like exotic flowers. Others swam with fins or flippers, or zoomed around by jet propulsion. To protect themselves from hungry predators, some used camouflage; others burrowed; still others swam faster or had bigger teeth and stronger jaws. Most managed to survive until the time came when their environment changed so dramatically that they couldn't cope—and they died out. Yet each time this happened, a whole new cast of characters appeared.

The very beginning of the Paleozoic era was trilobite time. In warm, shallow seas throughout the world, these little animals lived and prospered. Their hard outer skeletons and jointed legs helped them to win out in the struggle for life. Some kinds of trilobites stayed partly buried in the mud at the bottom of the ocean; others shuffled along the sea floor; still others swam or floated in the water above. Many trilobites, when threatened, could curl up in a ball for protection.

The fossil record shows that the first fish also appeared at the beginning of the Paleozoic era. They were pretty weird looking. Weighted down by scales and heavy bony plates, they swam slowly along the bottom of the sea, grubbing their food from the mud or straining it from the water. They had no jaws or teeth.

Later in the Paleozoic, fish with jaws appeared. These more modern animals were also equipped with a pair of fins that helped them to swim better. But it wasn't until the Mesozoic era that fish as we know them today came into being. Since Mesozoic times, the world's fish population has grown and diversified. In fact, modern fish are one of the world's most successful animal groups.

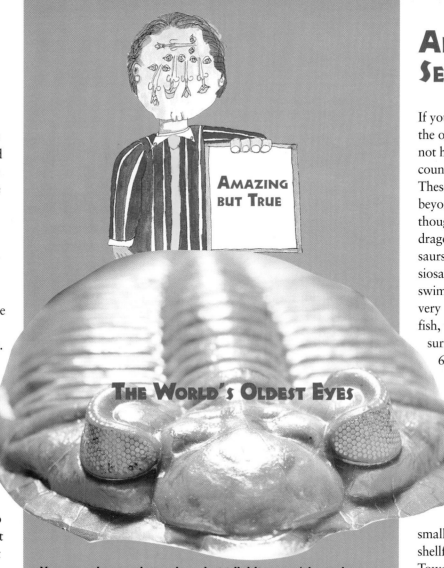

AMAZING BUT TRUE

THE WORLD'S OLDEST EYES

Your eyes have only one lens, but trilobite eyes (shown here greatly enlarged) had many separate lenses packed together. When a trilobite looked at something, it saw many different images of that thing at once, each from a slightly different angle.

How do we know about trilobite eyes? Unlike the soft eyes of most animals, trilobite eyes had hard lenses, made of a mineral called *calcite*. This meant that the eyes sometimes made it into the fossil record. They are, in fact, the oldest eyes known. To celebrate this fact, the museum has created a special device that allows you to see yourself as a trilobite would . . . if it could!

ANCIENT SEA DRAGONS

If you're ever out in a boat on the open sea, one thing you will not have to worry about is encountering a giant sea dragon. These creatures failed to make it beyond the Mesozoic era. Although they're often called "sea dragons," ichthyosaurs, mosasaurs (shown below), and plesiosaurs were actually giant swimming reptiles. They were very fast swimmers, but unlike fish, they had to come up to the surface to breathe air. About 65 million years ago, all of them died out. Exactly what went wrong remains a mystery, although scientists have made some good guesses. Mosasaurs, with their sharp, cone-shaped teeth, were always eating: smaller mosasaurs, sea turtles, shellfish, and other tasty things. Towards the end of the Mesozoic, because of changes in the climate and their environment, they probably couldn't find enough food to satisfy their huge appetites.

WHERE DINOSAURS STILL RULE!

Some were bigger than a tractor trailer truck. A few were smaller than an alley cat. For about 160 million years they ruled the earth. Then 65 million years ago ("mya") they disappeared in the most mysterious extinction ever.

We know them from the bones and teeth and footprints they left behind all over the world. The best loved and the most famous of all the animals that ever lived, they were the dinosaurs.

And when it comes to dinosaurs, the National Museum of Natural History has one of the most impressive collections you'll see anywhere. While dinosaur remains have been found in many parts of the world, most of the skeletons in this exhibition belong to dinosaurs who lived in the United States and western Canada.

Of the three big eras of prehistoric time—Paleozoic, Mesozoic, and Cenozoic—the age of reptiles came in the middle: the Mesozoic era. Although other animals lived then too, throughout most of the Mesozoic, the reptiles—dinosaurs, pterosaurs, and sea dragons—ruled.

THE GREAT DINOSAUR COVERUP

All over the world enormous dinosaur fossils lay buried in the earth, but people didn't know it. In fact, it took humans about 2.5 million years to come to the realization that dinosaurs once existed! The first fossil ever identified as a dinosaur was found in Great Britain in about 1822. Before that time, when someone found a dinosaur bone they assumed it was something else—part of an ancient giant bird, for instance.

In 1856 Dr. Joseph Leidy published the first description of dinosaur fossils in the United States. Two years later the first almost complete skeleton of a dinosaur found in this country was dug up in New Jersey, and described by Leidy.

AMAZING BUT TRUE

MONARCHS OF THE MESOZOIC

PALEOZOIC		
MESOZOIC		
CRETACEOUS (144-66.4 mya)	JURASSIC (208-144 mya)	TRIASSIC (245-208 mya)
CENOZOIC		

The Mesozoic era is divided into three major time periods: Cretaceous, Jurassic, and Triassic. Altogether these three time periods covered about 185 million years.

During the Mesozoic, the earth's surface underwent many dramatic changes. At the beginning, the continents were packed together into one big land mass. Then they gradually drifted apart, so that by the end of the Mesozoic, they resembled the arrangement we are familiar with today. As these changes happened, the climate and geography also changed, altering the kinds of plants that could grow. And all of the animals, including the dinosaurs, had to adapt to these changes too. Then, 65 million years ago, at the end of the Mesozoic, all the dinosaurs mysteriously died out.

What caused the dinosaurs' extinction? No one knows for sure. Many scientists think the combination of Earth's changes became too much for the animals to adjust to. Whatever the cause, the dinosaurs were not the only animals to die out as the Mesozoic era came to a close. It was around the same time that the flying reptiles and most of the giant sea reptiles disappeared too.

BE A DINOSAUR DETECTIVE!

As you look at the museum's dinosaur exhibits, you can play dinosaur detective much as museum scientists do. By taking a close look at dinosaurs' teeth and bones, you can figure out what they ate, how they moved around, and how they defended themselves. Here are some things to look for:

Jaws and Teeth
Most dinosaurs ate plants, but some ate flesh. The flesh-eaters had long, sharp teeth, often with saw-like edges.

Their jaws were usually bigger than those of plant-eaters, too. The teeth of plant-eaters were relatively short and flat, with broad, shearing surfaces.

Legs
All the flesh-eating dinosaurs walked only on their hind legs, as did some of the plant-eaters. Other plant-eaters walked on all fours, but even those, such as huge *Diplodocus,* may have reared up on their hind legs from time to time. Some two-legged walkers were slow, while others sped along at up to 43 kilometers (27 miles) per hour! Four-legged dinosaurs, with their huge, pillar-like legs, all lumbered along slowly.

Front Legs
All two-legged walkers had short front legs. These "arms" could be equipped with hands, hooves, fingers, or just with claws. Most dinosaurs with fingers could use them for gathering food, catching prey, and holding onto things. Some dinosaurs also used their front legs for defense.

Claws
Flesh-eating dinosaurs often had sharp, hooked claws for defense and for attacking and pulling apart their prey. Plant-eaters had broader, flatter claws and hooves, which could be used to scrape and dig for food.

Tails
Dinosaur tails came in many shapes, from short and thick to long and thin. Most two-legged walkers used their tails to help them balance. Some of the plant-eaters probably used their tails, equipped with clubs or whip-like extensions, for defense.

Far left: One of the museum's dinosaur detectives—a curator of paleobiology—with some dinosaur "puzzle pieces." Left: Fierce *Tyrannosaurus rex* pursues a smaller dinosaur.

Getting to Know *Diplodocus*

Working only from teeth and bones, scientists have been able to figure out a lot about *Diplodocus*. When all its bones are assembled, it's clear that *Diplodocus* was one of the largest dinosaurs. The skeleton in the Dinosaur Hall measures 22.5 meters (72 feet, 3 inches) from its nose to the tip of its tail. *Diplodocus* stood on all fours, with legs like pillars designed to bear its tremendous weight. Its head was very small, at the end of an extremely long neck, and its teeth, at the front of its mouth, were thin and pencil-like.

What can dinosaur detectives figure out from these basic facts? They know from its teeth that *Diplodocus* ate only plants —never animal flesh. And they know from the way the jaws work that this dinosaur could not chew its food. The teeth simply raked in leaves and conifer needles, and *Diplodocus* swallowed them whole. Finally, they know from the way the bones fit together that *Diplodocus's* neck was not just long, but also strong and flexible.

These facts allow some pretty good guesses about how *Diplodocus* lived. First of all, it probably used its long neck to reach treetop food that other dinosaurs couldn't get (as well as food on the ground and in the water). Second, since *Diplodocus* didn't chew before swallowing, it must have needed help digesting its tough, prickly food. Maybe, scientists suggest, this dinosaur swallowed stones. In its stomach, these stones would help to grind up the food. (Does this sound like a bizarre theory? This is exactly what birds do, which is where scientists got the idea.)

How did *Diplodocus* defend itself against meat-eating dinosaurs? Scientists think *Diplodocus* lived in herds, the way elephants do today. Sticking together, they would have had a better chance to defend their young, the sick, and the aged.

The Duckbill—Saved by its Teeth?

Towards the end of the Mesozoic era, there lived a whole group of dinosaurs with long, flat snouts. These were the "duckbilled dinosaurs," also called *hadrosaurs*. The duckbills walked on two legs and had tails flattened side to side. Many sported fancy crests. Inside each duckbill's mouth was row upon row of up to 700 diamond-shaped teeth, which continued to grow, fall out, and be replaced by new teeth throughout the animal's life. In the 1890s, scientists discovered two unusually complete duckbill fossils, including the remains of food in the animals' stomachs. The food was pine needles, twigs, seeds, and other land plants. What conclusions can you, as a dinosaur detective, draw from this evidence? Hadrosaurs were plant-eaters, certainly; and their upright posture suggests they spent most of their time on land. Scientists think the duckbills used their amazing teeth to grind and chew leaves and stems. Other plant-eating dinosaurs could only slice and chop their food—which was far less efficient. Maybe being able to eat things that other dinosaurs couldn't helped them to survive. Of all the dinosaurs, the duckbills were among the very last to die out. By the end of the Mesozoic duckbills, along with the closely-related horned dinosaurs, made up about 90 percent of all the large plant-eaters left on Earth.

Triceratops was another four-legged plant-eater of spectacular bulk. Its huge head took up nearly one-third of its body length. Its armored face had three sharp horns and a curved, parrot-like beak, and it was further protected by a bony frill shielding its thick, short neck.

Is It a Plane? Is It a Bird?

No, It's *Quetzalcoatlus!*

That large winged creature you see suspended in motionless flight over the Dinosaur Hall is not a bird—and certainly not an airplane. Rather, it's *Quetzalcoatlus,* one of several kinds of flying reptiles (known as *pterosaurs)* that lived during the age of the dinosaurs.

Some smaller pterosaurs were no bigger than a sparrow. But *Quetzalcoatlus,* with a wingspan of about 11 meters (35 feet), was the largest animal that ever flew.

The creature you see on exhibit is a model, not the real thing! It was made by museum workers from balsa wood and hollow steel, covered with fabric and then painted. It's been hanging there since 1981, when the renovated Dinosaur Hall opened to visitors.

AMAZING BUT TRUE

"Ancient Wing"

During the age of reptiles, the first birds appeared. The oldest known fossil bird is one called *Archaeopteryx,* which means "ancient wing."

In the Dinosaur Hall you can see the cast of a limestone slab bearing a fossil of this peculiar creature. It has some features you certainly won't see in any of the pigeons or sea gulls out on the Mall—or in any other living bird, for that matter!

Archaeopteryx's teeth, its long bony tail, and its three clawed fingers are all non-birdlike features that scientists say suggest that it had a distant reptilian ancestor—a flesh-eating dinosaur.

Did birds evolve from dinosaurs way back when? Scientists think that yes, they did. In fact, they say there's even a very good chance that birds are really fancy dinosaurs.

THE MAMMALS MOVE TO CENTER STAGE

Mammals today live all over the world and come in a great many shapes and sizes. Some of them are the largest animals we have. But this was not always so.

In the days of the dinosaurs, mammals were small and nocturnal (active at night). They stayed in the background, out of the dinosaurs' way. Then 65 million years ago the dinosaurs died out. With their rivals gone, many of the mammals that were already around evolved into much bigger descendants. Hundreds of new kinds appeared.

Both plant-eating and flesh-eating mammals evolved, as well as some omnivores, which means "everything eaters." All of this happened quite rapidly, during the early part of the Cenozoic era.

The exhibit called Mammals in the Limelight tells this story. Fossil skeletons have been placed in front of murals showing what scientists think the animals may have looked like in the wild. The exhibit is arranged chronologically (from earlier to later in time), so that you can see how different mammals evolved. For example, the earliest recognizable ancestor of the modern horse appeared about 55 million years ago. Known to science as Hyracotherium (hyrax beast), it had feet with four toes in front and three toes behind, and was only the size of a fox terrier. By about 36 million years ago, Mesohippus (middle horse) had arrived, a horse the size of a German Shepherd dog, with only three toes on each foot. By about 8 million years ago, horses had come to look pretty much as they do today, with one large toe, called a hoof, on each foot. Their hooves were designed to help them run on hard ground. They also had developed strong, slender legs for running fast and jaws and teeth suited to grazing.

Over almost 50 million years, as the murals show you, horses changed a lot, becoming adapted to living in a herd, feeding on coarse grasses, and escaping from predators with short bursts of speed.

ASK THE EXPERTS

♦ ♦ ♦ ABOUT MAMMALS

What are mammals, anyway?
They're warm-blooded animals with backbones and hair, which give birth to live babies (instead of hatching them out of eggs), and which feed their young with milk from the mother's own body. The group includes people, as well as a wide variety of other animals, ranging in size from shrews to elephants. Most mammals live on land; but whales, dolphins, and sea cows are mammals that live in the water.

THE 35-MILLION-YEAR-OLD SQUIRREL

Protosciurus is the oldest-known member of the squirrel family. It lived during the Oligocene epoch of the Cenozoic era (35 to 23 million years ago). Its bones are very similar to those of living tree squirrels. In fact, you probably would not notice anything strange if you were to look out your window right now and see *Protosciurus* in a nearby tree!

A modern squirrel

Left: These Przewalski's horses are rare modern-day relatives of early mammals whose skeletons are on display in the museum.

Amazing Ice Age Mammals

Don't Miss It!

One of the most eventful times in Earth's history was the Pleistocene epoch of the Cenozoic era. Compared to the age of reptiles, the Pleistocene happened the day before yesterday: from about 1.5 million to about 10,000 years ago. During the Pleistocene, there were at least four times when ice covered much of the world's land. Enormous sheets of ice (called glaciers) moved down from the North Pole to cover large sections of Europe, Asia, and North America. These glacial episodes, each lasting thousands of years, were followed by warmer intervals, also lasting thousands of years, when the glaciers melted and shrank. Early in the Pliocene epoch (5.2-1.6 mya), the first human beings evolved in Africa. Then gradually people moved to other parts of the world. Fossil evidence shows that by about 15,000 years ago, Ice Age people were roaming the plains and forests here in North America, hunting enormous mammals with stone-pointed spears.

The Ice Age Mammals hall contains a magnificent array of these giant mammals, including the woolly mammoth, an early relative of today's elephant. The "woolly" was covered with a thick coat of fur, two layers deep, to withstand the freezing cold and wet climate of Alaska and northern Eurasia. The coarse, shaggy outer layer repelled rain and snow; the soft, woolly inner layer provided extra warmth.

The fossil record tells us when the woolly mammoth became extinct. Thousands of woolly mammoth bones dating from earlier than 10,000 years ago have been found in Alaska and Siberia. The record stops after about 4000 years ago. Was hunting by humans the cause of the woolly mammoth's extinction? Scientists think not. The woolly disappeared rapidly after the last Ice Age ended. With the warmer weather, food supplies, living space, and other conditions changed—and it seems likely the woolly mammoth could not adjust.

In the Ice Age Mammals hall, you can compare the teeth of the woolly mammoth with those of another extinct elephant, the mastodon. While both of these animals were plant-eaters, they ate different *kinds* of plants. The difference is reflected in their teeth and jaws. Two lower jaws with teeth are there for you to touch—and compare.

STICKY PITS

During the Pleistocene, the area that is now downtown Los Angeles, California, was a very different place. There were no palm trees—and, of course, no movie stars! Instead a variety of now-extinct animals inhabited the region's thick pine forests. Streams ran through the forests, and at one place in particular, hot oil and gas continually bubbled up through the sandy bottoms of the streambeds to collect in pools. Sometimes the streams would dry up, and the oil in the pools would congeal into sticky tar. Leaves and other debris would then cover up the streambeds, hiding the tar.

Every once in a while, an animal would wander in, get stuck in the tar, and die. Then other animals would come to feed on the dead animal, and they too would get stuck and die. Gradually the carcasses of these animals sank farther and farther into the tar until they were completely covered up. By sealing out water and air, the tar preserved the bones. For several thousand years, in that one place, more and more animals kept dying and getting buried in this same way.

Since 1913, scientists from the Los Angeles Museum of Natural History have been excavating the site, which is no longer sticky and is now called the La Brea Tar Pits. They've found thousands and thousands of bones belonging to 200 different kinds of animals. In the Ice Age Mammals hall, you can see the skeletons of some of the most interesting of these animals.

Creatures from the Pits
Dire wolf
The most common animal found in the tar pits is the dire wolf, which was a lot like wolves of today but slower moving and not as intelligent. Dire wolves travelled in packs, exhausting their prey on long chases. Over the course of several thousand years, more than 1600 of them got stuck in the tar pits and died.

Inset: The skull of an ancient saber-toothed cat. The painting shows an artist's conception of what downtown Los Angeles looked like 36,000 years ago.

Saber-toothed cat
With long, sharp teeth and jaws that were hinged to open extra wide, the saber-toothed cat would grab its prey, stab it, rip open its throat, and then eat it. Sabertooths died out when the large animals they preyed on, such as the ground sloth, became extinct.

Ground sloth
Ungainly and slow-moving, the ground sloth was a plant eater. Some kinds grazed in open country, some browsed in trees. One of its biggest enemies was the saber-toothed cat. Thick skin fortified with bony lumps was the main protection for one of the three families of ground sloths.

DON'T MISS IT!

After you finish seeing the Ice Age mammals, you'll want to visit Great Mammals of North America, which has dioramas showing —in their natural habitats—twelve different mammals that survived the Ice Age and are still living today.

MEET THE FLOCK

Remember *Archaeopteryx*, the first known bird, from the days of the dinosaurs? (His picture is on p. 35.) Well, you can meet his descendants—by the dozens and dozens—in the museum's first-floor Bird hall.

In the wild, birds are fun to watch because of their bright colors and lively habits. In the museum, you have to imagine their lively habits. However, one advantage of looking at museum birds is that you can get a lot closer to them than you can get to birds in the wild. This means you can study certain things about them—like their bills and feet—for clues as to how they lived. You can also see *more kinds* of birds here than in any one place in the wild. In fact, in the Bird hall you can see hundreds of different species, exotic and familiar, from all over the world.

Passenger pigeons are a type of bird that is now extinct. This is "Martha," the last survivor of her kind, who died in captivity in 1914.

Every bird has a bill made of strong, lightweight material somewhat like your fingernails. The shape and size of the bill depends on what the bird eats. The male rhinoceros hornbill, for instance, uses his long, pointed bill to pass insects and fruits to his mate and offspring, who stay walled inside their mud nest until the young are old enough to leave. The female receives food with her bill, and also uses it to break free from the nest when the time is right.

AMAZING BUT TRUE

ON THEIR TOES

Birds' feet come in many shapes and sizes, with their toes arranged in different ways. For example, the chickadee's foot, with three toes in front and one in back, is especially designed for perching. The woodpecker's foot, with two toes in front and two in back, is perfectly suited to climbing up tree trunks. A duck's paddle-shaped foot, with webbing between the toes, is excellent for swimming.

Right: The museum's vast egg collection, stored behind the scenes, is of great value for research.

Born to Fly

If you were a bird, flying would be as easy as breathing in and out. You'd spread your wings to catch the wind. Raise your tail. Push off with your feet. Flap your wings. And off you'd go!

Once airborne and flying fast enough, you'd glide for a while with your wings and tail outspread. Flapping and gliding, flapping and gliding, you'd sail through the air. A tilt of your tail to the right or the left, and you could steer in any direction you wanted to go. To return to earth, you'd simply lower your tail and glide on in, with wings outstretched, landing on your feet.

Like a well-built machine, a bird's whole body is designed for flight. Bird wings are thicker in the middle, so that their top surface is curved more than their underside. This shape is called an *airfoil,* and it takes advantage of a natural force called *lift* that allows a bird—or an airplane, for that matter—to take flight. (For more about lift, see p. 115.) A bird flaps its wings, powered by large strong muscles, to move itself forward.

Birds with short, rounded wings are good at turning sharply in tight places. Birds with long, pointed wings are fast long-distance fliers. Birds with big, broad wings are skilled at soaring and swooping.

Only birds have feathers. A swan has about 25,000, while even a tiny hummingbird has about 1,000. Some of them are special "flight feathers," which increase the wings' flapping effect. The stiff feathers of a bird's tail can be opened and closed like a fan, or tilted from side to side. Other feathers give a bird's body a smooth, streamlined shape to cut through the air. They also keep the bird from losing body heat, so it can conserve its energy for flight.

Unlike most land animals, a bird's bones are mostly hollow. Instead of heavy jaws and teeth, a bird has only a beak or bill. This lightweight frame means that a bird can use less energy to stay up in the air.

So there you have it! From the tip of its beak to the end of its tail, a bird's whole body is designed to fly.

WONDERS UNDER THE SEA

If you've ever gone snorkeling or traveled in a glass-bottomed boat, you've had a glimpse of the astounding variety of life that exists in the world's oceans. The exhibition called Exploring Marine Ecosystems re-creates some living ocean communities, including, near the entrance, a reconstructed kelp forest from Maine. It's 9 meters (30 feet) deep, and filled with kelp plants (a kind of large brown seaweed), sea stars, lobsters, and other members of this ecosystem's food web.

Two model ecosystems allow you to compare the differences between a tropical coral reef from the Caribbean Ocean and the conditions on the rocky Atlantic coast of Maine. The colorful residents of the warm-water coral reef tank include living corals; crabs; blue-green, green, and red algae; brilliant parrot-fish, and tangs (a colorful group of fishes also known as "butterfly fish"). In contrast, the cold-water tank contains kelp, marsh grass, lobsters, scallops, mussels, hake, and tomcod (the last two are related to the common codfish).

Both of these re-creations are based on more than 25 years of research by a Smithsonian scientist. As the tanks are allowed to develop naturally, the scientists studying them are gaining a better understanding of how natural ocean communities function. In the meantime, you get the chance to study them up close—without ever getting wet!

Top: A sea fan

Middle: Feather duster worms

Bottom: Elkhorn coral

The small fish "swimming" across the page are queen angelfish. The larger fish is a damselfish.

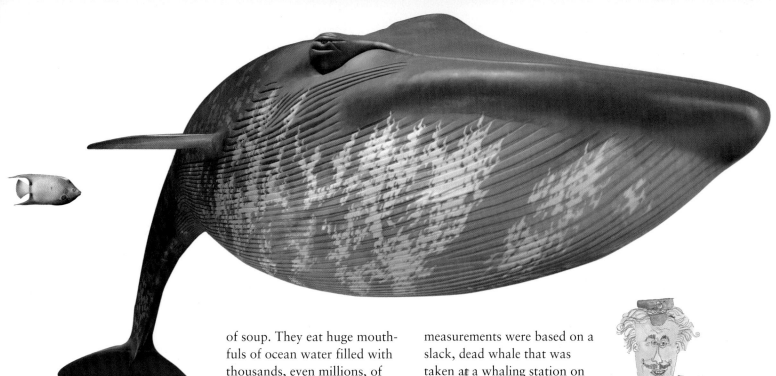

A TALE OF A WHALE

The largest single exhibit in the whole Natural History Museum is a huge, fiberglass model of a blue whale in the Sea Life hall. The blue whale is the biggest animal that has ever lived on Earth, even bigger than the dinosaurs. Some blue whales are more than 30 meters (100 feet) long, and can weigh more than 136,000 kilograms (300,000 pounds). Yet these enormous creatures have no teeth, and their food is a kind of soup. They eat huge mouthfuls of ocean water filled with thousands, even millions, of tiny creatures such as sardines, krill (which look like miniature shrimp), and plankton.

The whale pushes these mouthfuls through rows of fringed plates inside its mouth which act like a sieve to catch the solids and spit out the water. As its mouth fills up with "soup," pleated folds in its throat balloon out to make room for the food. Since a whale's throat takes up almost half its body length, a whale that's dining has quite a different body shape from a whale between meals.

This difference has caused the museum some embarrassment. Its blue whale model was made many years ago. Its measurements were based on a slack, dead whale that was taken at a whaling station on the island of South Georgia. Nowadays, better diving equipment and small undersea submarines take human beings into the oceans to watch and photograph living whales. We've learned that, supported by the water, whales look much slimmer and more streamlined than the museum's model. From time to time, there's talk of taking the model down because its shape isn't right. However, some biologists point out that the model isn't completely wrong, either. They say that it's about the shape a blue whale would be if it still had half a mouthful of food at the end of a meal!

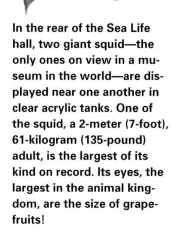

In the rear of the Sea Life hall, two giant squid—the only ones on view in a museum in the world—are displayed near one another in clear acrylic tanks. One of the squid, a 2-meter (7-foot), 61-kilogram (135-pound) adult, is the largest of its kind on record. Its eyes, the largest in the animal kingdom, are the size of grapefruits!

NATIVE AMERICANS

Long before the coming of the European settlers, American Indians lived in all parts of what is now the United States. As you will see in this exhibition, *how* these people lived depended in part on *where* they lived. The houses they lived in, the food they ate, and the clothes they wore varied a lot from place to place. Here's an example from the Plains Indians.

A Home for All Seasons

Blazing hot in summer. Freezing cold in winter. Heavy rains. High winds. Fierce blizzards. Even tornadoes! These were just some of the weather conditions that the tipi used by Native Americans of the Plains had to withstand. It also had to be lightweight and portable because, about a hundred years ago, these people moved around a lot. They were following the buffalo herds they hunted for food, clothing, and shelter. Yet through it all, the tipi remained a cozy home for all seasons.

Here is how the design of the tipi worked:

◆ Every tipi had a frame of wooden poles and a cover made of sturdy buffalo skins. In the winter, the bottom edge of the cover was weighted down with rocks to help keep out the wind. In the summer, the cover could be rolled up part way to let the breezes in.

◆ Notice, on the top of the tipi, two flaps sticking up like ears. These are the smoke flaps. In between the smoke flaps is a hole to let out smoke from a fireplace inside the tipi. To keep wind and rain out of the fire, the smoke flaps could be adjusted from the inside, using two wooden poles.

◆ Instead of being a perfect cone, every tipi was built to tilt slightly. This angled position, along with an anchor rope, helped to keep the tipi from blowing over, even in high winds.

Left: This Sioux chief's bonnet from 1880 contains 77 eagle feathers.

Below: A 100-year-old Arapaho tipi. In a real Plains Indian village, it would have been part of a large circle of tipis.

BEHIND THE SCENES
THE BONE DETECTIVE

Douglas Ubelaker is the FBI's top bone consultant. He has been involved in more than 500 of their cases, helping to identify remains, find evidence of foul play, and determine what kind of weapon was used in murders. But his real passion is studying the bones of people who died so long ago that no records remain of who they were and how they lived. Dr. Ubelaker is curator of physical anthropology at the National Museum of Natural History. Physical anthropology is the science of how human beings have evolved over many thousands of years and how their physical characteristics differ from one part of the world to another.

Sometimes Ubelaker makes surprising connections between people of long ago and those of today. While studying the bones of ancient Ecuadorean Indians, he noticed odd bumps on the bones of their feet where the toes attached. He found that only one group of people in the modern world have bumps like this—short people who work in offices! Why? If office workers sit in chairs that are too high for them, they bend their toes into a "tiptoe" position so that their feet can touch the floor. But what about the ancient Ecuadorean Indians? They probably carried out a lot of their daily tasks on the ground in a kneeling position—with their toes bent under them.

Ubelaker recently examined bones from eighteen graves excavated from a mid-seventeenth century colonial settlement in Maryland. Without headstones, church records, or any other clues, he was still able to discover a great deal about these people and their lives. He could tell that most of the colonists had died young—the average age for the men was thirty-one, and for the women, thirty-six. Even so, many had brittle, diseased bones that are usually seen today only in old people. Ubelaker thinks their bone disease may have been caused by aspects of their harsh life. The push, pull, and strain of physical work leaves marks on the bones—and the men of the settlement showed signs of having labored very hard. About a quarter of the colonists had suffered broken bones at some time in their lives. Many of the colonists—even one who was only about thirteen years old when he died—smoked clay pipes, leaving tobacco stains and wear marks in their teeth.

Although the Maryland colonists died so long ago that no one even knows their names, Dr. Ubelaker tries not to forget that the bones he studies were once living, feeling people.

DISCOVERY ROOM

The first-floor Discovery Room is designed especially for you! Here's your chance to experience at first hand some of the things you've been seeing on your walk through the museum. You can touch a geode . . . count the rattles on a rattlesnake . . . feel the smooth, rounded cusps of a mastodon tooth . . . try on clothes from around the world . . . and much more!

Special shelves along one wall hold "Discovery Boxes" on interesting topics. For example, there are boxes on dolls, on reptiles and amphibians, on toys from different countries, on rocks, and on seashells. Inside the boxes are objects that you can take out and examine as a museum scientist would.

The Discovery Room is open to the public from 10:30 a.m. to 3:30 p.m. on Saturday and Sunday, and from noon to 2:30 p.m. on weekdays.

HISS, CHIRP, RATTLE, CLICK!

Tucked away in a corner on the second floor is an exhibition featuring the most successful animals on Earth, in living, breathing, moving, *noisy* color. It's called the O. Orkin Insect Zoo. If you are intrigued by the thought of a world in miniature, where you can pet a hissing cockroach, hold a caterpillar pupa in the palm of your hand, watch a tarantula eat its supper, or crawl through a termite mound, then this is the place for you!

Insects live all over the world. In the coldest stretches of ice and tundra, the swiftest rivers, the busiest city streets, the deepest, darkest bogs and the hottest, driest deserts, you can find insects. Scientists estimate that these tiny creatures make up nearly 90 percent of all animal life. There are about 200 million insects for every human being alive today!

Insects have been on Earth for more than 380 million years, longer than most animals we are familiar with today. Gradually, down through the ages, millions of different *species* (kinds) of insects have evolved. Each species has developed special traits that adapt it to the environment it lives in.

In the Insect Zoo, you can watch insects and their relatives in natural settings of pond, desert, mangrove swamp, tropical rainforest, and a Washington, D.C., backyard. You can see how they grow from egg to adult, feed themselves, deal with danger, and even make themselves at home in your home!

This strange-looking creature is a weevil— shown much larger than life-size! It bores into stems, roots, and seeds to lay eggs, doing great damage to crops.

Is It an Insect . . . or Something Else?

Not every tiny creature that crawls or hops is an insect. If you're in doubt, count its legs. If there are six, it's an insect. If there are more or less than six, it is probably some other kind of arthropod. Other arthropods include millipedes (thousand-leggers), centipedes (hundred-leggers), crustaceans (such as crabs), and spiders.

The group of animals to which insects and their closest relatives belong is called *Arthropoda*. The animals in this group are alike in several important ways. Instead of having an internal skeleton as you and I do, all arthropods have bodies that are held together by a stiff outside skeleton. As an arthropod grows bigger, it sheds its skin, revealing a new and better one. All arthropods also have jointed legs which, depending on the creature, may be used for walking, swimming, crawling, hopping, or grabbing prey.

Amazing But True
Munch, Crunch, Sip

What do insects eat? Practically everything! Wine bottle corks, blood, fence posts, fruits and vegetables, tobacco, glue, other insects—you name it, and some insect or another is likely to favor it as a steady diet. As you look around the Insect Zoo, you'll notice that some insects—like caterpillars and beetles—eat only solid food. Others—like milkweed bugs and acacia ants—stick entirely to a liquid diet.

By taking a very close look, you might also notice that the mouthparts of these insects are perfectly designed to suit their eating habits. For example, caterpillars have tiny jaws that move back and forth and from side to side while munching. Acacia ants have straw-like structures they use for sipping.

Because of the great variety of things they eat, insects can feed in many different places. This means different kinds of insects do not have to compete for the same food.

FROM THE REAL ESTATE OFFICE OF I.M.A. BUGG:

To share: Furnished house. Warm, tropical setting all year. Unlimited food supply. No major predators. Spacious, packed closets. Big backyard. Countless nooks and crannies. Sedate, warm-blooded pets. Damp basement full of rotting wood beams. Plenty of room for a growing family. No appointment necessary.

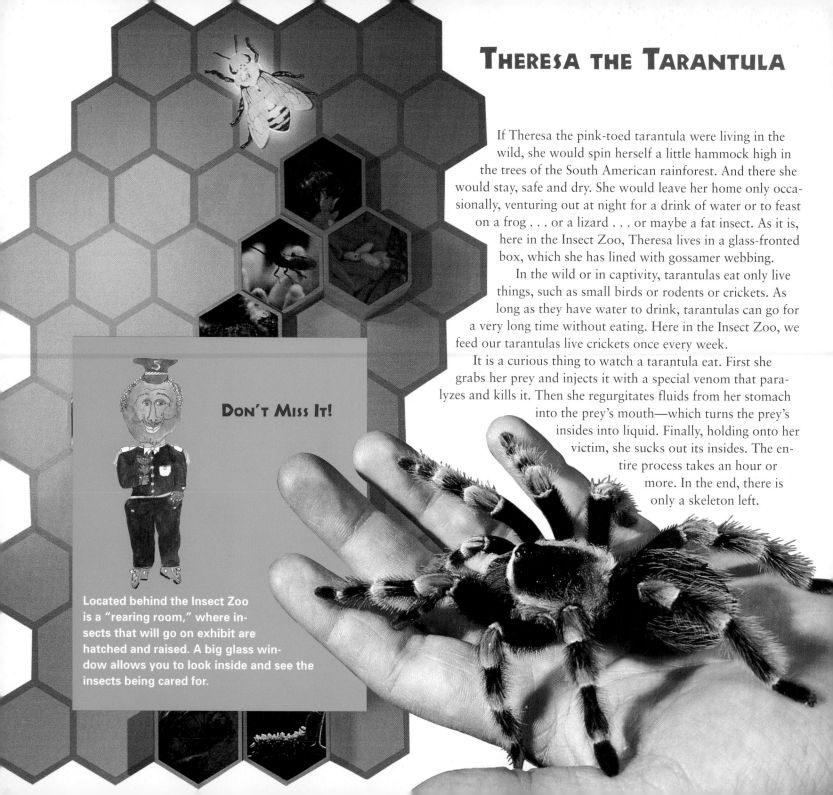

THERESA THE TARANTULA

If Theresa the pink-toed tarantula were living in the wild, she would spin herself a little hammock high in the trees of the South American rainforest. And there she would stay, safe and dry. She would leave her home only occasionally, venturing out at night for a drink of water or to feast on a frog . . . or a lizard . . . or maybe a fat insect. As it is, here in the Insect Zoo, Theresa lives in a glass-fronted box, which she has lined with gossamer webbing.

In the wild or in captivity, tarantulas eat only live things, such as small birds or rodents or crickets. As long as they have water to drink, tarantulas can go for a very long time without eating. Here in the Insect Zoo, we feed our tarantulas live crickets once every week.

It is a curious thing to watch a tarantula eat. First she grabs her prey and injects it with a special venom that paralyzes and kills it. Then she regurgitates fluids from her stomach into the prey's mouth—which turns the prey's insides into liquid. Finally, holding onto her victim, she sucks out its insides. The entire process takes an hour or more. In the end, there is only a skeleton left.

DON'T MISS IT!

Located behind the Insect Zoo is a "rearing room," where insects that will go on exhibit are hatched and raised. A big glass window allows you to look inside and see the insects being cared for.

HANDS ON, HANDS OFF!

Male cockroaches from Madagascar can grow to as long as 10 centimeters (4 inches), bigger than a mouse! They have thick horns behind their heads, which they use in fighting one another ferociously, head to head, while making loud hissing noises. While you're in the Insect Zoo, don't forget to ask if you can see—and pet—our very own hissing cockroach from Madagascar.

The head of the cone-headed grasshopper is filled with muscles used to move its jaws. These jaws are so powerful that this tiny animal has been known to bite right into a person's finger when given a chance. In the Insect Zoo, you can see a cone-headed grasshopper close up—but you needn't worry about your fingers. Here these animals are kept safely behind glass!

A *very* close-up view of a cone-headed grasshopper.

TO BEE OR NOT TO BEE

As a little girl in Wisconsin, she wandered through farmland finding insects, identifying them, and storing her treasures in old cigar boxes. Today, as an entomologist (a scientist who studies insects), Dr. Beth Norden of the Smithsonian's Department of Entomology is still wandering and collecting. But now she deposits her specimens in the National Insect Collection, where scientists from around the world can study them.

There are more types of insects than of any other creatures on Earth. Many species have never been studied or even named. So much remains to be learned! But entomologists don't just gather new insects. They also spend many hours organizing and examining the insects they have already collected. They sort insects, pin them, prepare alcohol vials and microscope slide mounts, place labels on them, and store them so that they can be found quickly when someone wants to study them.

Dr. Norden's area of interest is pollination, so she studies wasps and bees. She especially enjoys looking at these stinging insects under the high magnification of a scanning electron

microscope. Then she can see ornate pollen grains caught in feathery hairs, and learn more about the insect's diet and what kinds of plants it visits. Although it is fascinating to see tiny features enlarged under the microscope, Dr. Norden likes studying live insects in the field even more.

While many people avoid insects with stingers, Dr. Norden seeks them out in a variety of habitats. Sometimes, however, she finds more than insects. Recently, while working in a tropical rainforest in Sri Lanka, she was surrounded by a troop of thirty macaque monkeys. As the females sat watching, the aggressive males rolled back their lips, displaying large, sharp teeth. Dr. Norden's only weapon was her insect net as they began taking turns running at her. Refusing to become monkey meat, she whacked them with her net pole as they charged. The frightening attack lasted almost thirty minutes before the monkeys tired, allowing her to escape their circle.

Even without angry monkeys, field work is always an adventure. It often gives Dr. Norden a chance to bring back living insects for the Insect Zoo. Since checked luggage undergoes extreme temperature and pressure changes, she has to hand carry insects onto the plane. Small insects can usually travel undetected in pill bottles or inside dirty socks. But once, as her purse passed through the security check, the attendant looked alarmed. "Madam, there's something moving inside," he gasped. In fact, Dr. Norden's purse was filled with large grasshoppers—nothing out of the ordinary for her. She smiled and replied, "I have the proper permits."

Far left: A photo of Dr. Beth Norden collecting Perdita bees in Ajo, Arizona, superimposed on a scanning electron microscope photo of pollen on bee hairs.

Above: An illustration of a Perdita bee sits atop an even more greatly magnified grain of pollen.

MYSTERIOUS MUMMIES UNDER WRAPS

Upstairs on the second floor, in a hall called Origins of Western Culture, you can find them. Mute and mysterious—Egyptian mummies from long ago. As we saw from the work of Doug Ubelaker (see p. 45), there's a lot scientists can learn from the bones and teeth of people who lived a very long time ago. So it was no wonder that Smithsonian researchers wanted to get a good look at the skeletons of three of the mummies in the museum's care.

But mummies are very fragile. If cut open, they might easily fall apart. So, the best way to see inside them is to use techniques commonly used with live human beings: X-rays and CAT scan images.

Three mummies—which have since been nicknamed Indiana Jones, Ancient Annie, and Minister Cox—were driven to George Washington University Medical Center. Inside the radiology examining rooms, they were positioned on special tables, just as any live patient would be—except that the technician didn't have to tell the mummies not to move around!

Indiana Jones went first. Lying under dim lights in the X-ray room, he was, to many who were watching, a less than pretty sight. His linen wrappings had mostly been removed, revealing a blackened, shrivelled-up body with some bones sticking through.

However, his skeleton was still intact—and it revealed to the researchers a number of things about him. His X-rays showed a narrow pelvis, triangular in shape—a sure sign he was a male. His pictures also showed teeth that had *some* wear and decay but not a whole lot, as well as bones that were fully mature with some arthritis. These clues told the researchers that he was in his mid-to-late thirties when he died. However, the cause of his death is still a mystery.

Ancient Annie followed Indiana Jones into the X-ray room. From the shape of her pelvis, which was wider (for childbearing) than a male pelvis would be, it was apparent that she was a female. Her X-rays also gave clues to her social status. They showed that during mummification linen padding had been placed under her skin to give her a more lifelike expression. This special treatment probably means that she came from a wealthy family. From the condition of her teeth and bones, the researchers were able to guess that she was in her mid-to-late twenties when she died.

The final mummy examined was Minister Cox. (He's named for the person who donated him to the museum, a former diplomat named Cox.) For this mummy, the more expensive CAT scan technology was used. This procedure can produce more detailed images than X-rays—and in 3-D.

One discovery about the minister was that his brain had been removed. If a person was important, the brain was removed during mummification—with an iron hook through the nostrils. This was a tricky and time-consuming procedure.

Other telling features in Minister Cox's remains included worn-down teeth and joints with arthritis—both signs of age. The researchers think he died in his mid-to-late forties—which in those days was considered fairly old.

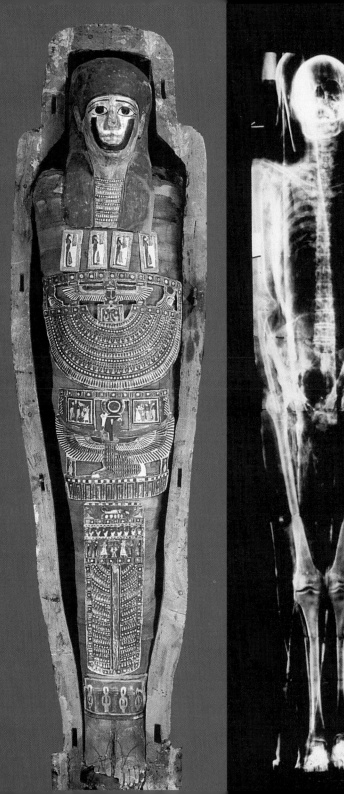

Left: The ancient Egyptians mummified animals as well as people—including bulls, cats, birds, and even crocodiles! This cat mummy is on display in the Origins of Western Culture hall.

Right: Minister Cox's mummy in its case

Far Right: An X-ray, showing the mummy's skeleton.

What exactly is a mummy?
A mummy is the preserved body—flesh and all—of a human being or some other kind of animal. Sometimes mummies were made accidentally by nature. For instance, they have been found buried in peat bogs. Sometimes, as in ancient Egypt, mummies were made on purpose.

Why did the ancient Egyptians mummify their dead?
For religious reasons. The Egyptians believed that the dead person's spirit would die if the body were allowed to rot away. To provide a home for the spirit, they preserved the body as much as possible.

How did they do it?
After washing the body, they would usually remove the internal organs and store them in containers called "canopic jars." Then they covered the body with special salts and let it dry out for about a month. Finally they coated it with resin (plant gum), wrapped it in linen, and placed it in a coffin. The whole process took about seventy days.

EARTHLY TREASURE

The museum's second-floor Janet Annenberg Hooker Hall of Geology, Gems and Minerals (opening 7/97) contains some of the most amazing treasures you'll ever see gathered in one place. In addition to rare and magnificent gems, there are huge quartz crystals from Africa, a natural sandstone "sculpture," and even a ring-shaped meteorite from outer space. Walk around a giant globe, watch a video in "Plate Tectonics Theater," and learn about the work of Smithsonian scientists in uncovering the fiery secrets of volcanoes.

Rocks: Earth's First Recyclers

If you've ever picked up a rock or a pebble to take a closer look, you'll be sure to enjoy the section of this hall called the Rocks Gallery. Here, through computer activities, you'll discover that rocks form in three basic ways: by magma (hot, semi-liquid rock from deep within the earth) cooling down and hardening into an igneous rock; by already-existing rock changing form and color as a result of heat and pressure to create a metamorphic rock; or by pebbles, sand, or other sediment hardening into a solid mass to create a sedimentary rock. You'll also learn that all rocks are made from basic natural substances called *minerals*. What's more, rocks keep recycling themselves. Heat from deep within the earth melts them; pressure from overlying rocks squeezes them; wind and water wear them down into sand and pebbles. As a result, new rocks are created from old ones over and over again. And this has been occurring ever since the earth was formed more than 4.6 billion years ago!

A crystal of the mineral spudomene, from California.

It's Earth Shaking!

As you walk around on "solid earth" you may be surprised to know that the rocks beneath your feet are actually moving! The earth's crust is made of brittle rock six to forty kilometers thick (four to twenty-five miles), broken into about a dozen giant pieces—and many smaller ones—called "plates." The plates carry the continents and ocean basins on top of them. As the plates float on the earth's slowly churning mantle, they sometimes bump and rub against one another. It is mainly in these areas of stress and friction that earthquakes and volcanoes occur.

Scientists say that over the past 4.6 billion years, this movement of the earth's plates—which they call plate tectonics—has resulted in many big changes. Continents have formed, moved apart, and joined together. Sea levels have risen and fallen. Mountains and lakes have formed and been destroyed. Climates have gotten colder and hotter, wetter and drier.

Crystals are some of the most beautiful objects in all of nature. Most crystals form when heat from deep inside the earth melts minerals in rocks. Then the minerals cool and harden into fancy shapes. Every crystal starts out as a tiny seed or baby crystal. It grows as atoms attach themselves to the seed and to one another, layer upon layer, in a regular pattern. Different minerals tend to take on different crystal shapes or "habits." Above are three specimens of the mineral Smithsonite.

AMAZING BUT TRUE
WHAT A GEM!

As spectacular as they are, diamonds, emeralds, and other gems are really just fancy cousins of everyday minerals. But that doesn't make them any less special. Take diamonds, for example. Diamonds are formed when carbon atoms bond together under extreme heat and pressure deep within the earth. After mining, raw diamonds are cut and polished to show off their radiant sparkle. The best, most expensive diamonds are very big and very clear. Most diamonds are white—but some especially rare ones are blue, yellow, pink, or red. In the National Gem Collection Gallery you can see the finest collection of colored diamonds on exhibit anywhere.

People are usually surprised when they see the Hope Diamond, not just because it's so big (it weighs 45.52 carats), but because it's a vivid dark blue. It's one of the most famous jewels in the world, although most of the stories about it are just that—stories. Anyone who owned it, according to the legend, came to a bad end. The last person who owned and wore the Hope Diamond was a wealthy American woman named Evalyn Walsh McLean. She did die—but only after wearing and enjoying the jewel for almost 40 years!

NATIONAL
MUSEUM OF
AMERICAN
HISTORY

WELCOME TO A WORLD OF TREASURES FROM THE PAST

NATIONAL MUSEUM OF AMERICAN HISTORY
**CONSTITUTION AVENUE BETWEEN 12TH AND 14TH STREETS, NW
MALL ENTRANCE (SHOWN AT LEFT): MADISON DRIVE BETWEEN 12TH
AND 14TH STREETS, NW**

In most families, there's someone who hates to throw anything out. Magazines, newspaper clippings and ticket stubs, letters and photographs, outgrown toys or out-of-fashion clothes are packed away in the basement, garage, or attic. Most kids love to poke around in old family treasures like this, finding their own baby clothes, or their father's football jacket, or the letters grandma wrote to grandpa when he was overseas in the war.

The National Museum of American History is like the "saver" in your family, but on a grand scale. It saves things for the whole country—more than 18 million objects, and the collection is still growing. Only a fraction of these things are on display at any one time, but even that will be enough to keep you busy for hours.

If Americans have used it, worn it, ridden on it, played with it, laughed or cried over it, it's probably in this museum. The museum groups these things in displays that explain who made or used them, and when, and why. Looking at them is like time traveling. In one room, it's just after the American Revolution; in another, it's 1950, and clunky room-sized computers are starting to change our world.

As a time traveler, you can really start anywhere. Most visitors, however, enter the museum from the Mall entrance, which opens onto the building's second floor. Straight ahead of you are two of the museum's biggest attractions. One is a famous, tattered flag. In front of the flag, you'll notice something else that always draws a crowd. When you get closer, you'll see what's in the hole between the first and second floors. You may have a hard time pulling yourself away, but there's lots more to see on your journey through time!

Where to Find It

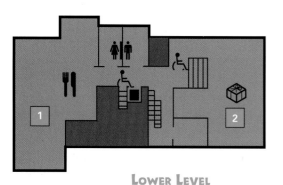

Lower Level

1 Cafeteria
2 Museum Shop and Bookstore

Note: Floorplans highlight kid-friendly attractions featured in this book. You can get a complete, up-to-date map at the Information Desk.

Constitution Avenue entrance

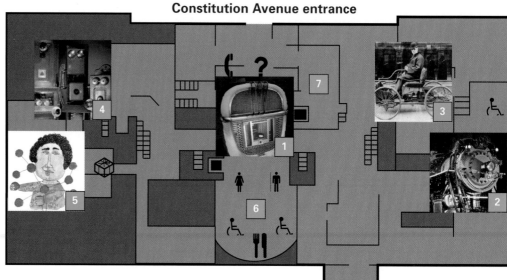

First Floor

Mall entrance

Second Floor

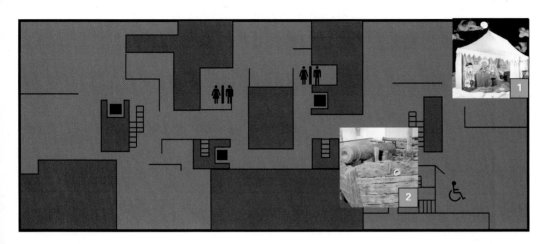

THIRD FLOOR

FIRST FLOOR

1 Material World
2 Railroad Hall
3 Road Transportation
4 Information Age
5 Science in American Life
6 Ice Cream Parlor
7 Carmichael Auditorium

SECOND FLOOR

1 Star-Spangled Banner Foucault Pendulum
2 First Ladies
3 After the Revolution
4 Hands on History Room
5 Field to Factory

THIRD FLOOR

1 Armed Forces
2 Gunboat *Philadelphia*

KEY TO SYMBOLS

? Information
Restrooms
Telephone
Accessible entrance
Elevator
Stairs/Escalator
Museum Shop
Food Service

INSIDER TIPS

◆ Guided tours leave at 10:00 a.m. and 1:00 p.m., Monday-Saturday, from the two Information Desks, located just inside the Mall and Constitution Avenue entrances. This book's tour starts on the Mall side, with the Star-Spangled Banner (number 1 on the second floor floorplan).

◆ At the Information Desks you can pick up a free brochure just for kids called "Hunt for History." The brochure has two versions—one for 6-to-9-year-olds and one for 10-to-13-year-olds. Both have clues that you can follow to find special objects in the museum; each hunt takes about one hour. Bring along a pen or pencil to write in your finds.

◆ On weekday and Saturday mornings look for roving Interpretive Carts on the first floor. Staffed by volunteers, the carts are on three different subjects: early sound recording, cotton ginning, and mystery artifacts (unusual items from the past that are hard to identify). All three carts give you a chance to pick things up, try them out, and get your questions answered.

Oh Say, Can You See?

One of the biggest stars in this museum is a very old American flag, made of fifteen cotton stars and fifteen wool stripes, sewn on a linen backing. It was hand sewn by Mary Pickersgill of Baltimore, Maryland, in 1815. Its stars and stripes stand for all the states of the union at that time. Little did Mary know that her humble creation would become the most famous flag in American history.

In 1814, the United States and Great Britain were at war. On the night of September 13, an American named Francis Scott Key watched from a boat in the Patapsco River as the British attacked Fort McHenry near Baltimore. The next morning, Key was relieved to see the American flag still flying over the fort. The sight of the flag—the one sewn by Mary Pickersgill—told him that the British attack had failed. Fort McHenry was still in American hands!

In fact, Francis Scott Key was so relieved that he sat down soon afterwards and told the story of the American victory in a poem. Later his poem was set to music and named "The Star-Spangled Banner."

The Smithsonian has owned the Star-Spangled Banner since 1912. For many years, it hung uncovered where it is now, in the museum's second-floor rotunda. After a while, though, the museum staff noticed that dust and light and air pollution were weakening the cotton and wool fibers. Something had to be done to rescue this important national treasure.

Museum workers cleaned the flag very gently with a special hand-held vacuum cleaner. Then they hung it behind a curtain for protection, showing it only once an hour for a few minutes. But even that eventually proved to be too much. Conservators are cleaning and restoring the flag again, while struggling with the question of how it should be displayed.

**AMAZING
BUT TRUE**

Before the Star-Spangeld Banner came to the Smithsonian, people had cut off pieces from its edge for souvenirs. As a result, the flag is now about 8 feet shorter than it was when Mary Pickersgill made it. The photo shows an overhead view of the Star-Spangled Banner with the Foucault Pendulum below it.

THE FOUCAULT PENDULUM

Want to see the earth rotate on its axis? You don't even have to leave the museum. Just join the crowd of onlookers at the Foucault (that's pronounced FOO-CO) pendulum. The 109-kilogram (240-pound) brass bob of the pendulum swings across a compass design set into a hole between the first and second floors. If you watch the pendulum for a few minutes, you'll notice that the line of the pendulum's swing seems to be moving clockwise. If you're there at the right time, you'll see the pendulum knock down one of the red pegs standing at the circumference of the circle. (That happens every twenty-four minutes.) But what's really happening? You and the museum and the city of Washington have rotated—in fact, the whole Earth has rotated—beneath the pendulum.

Many people who see the pendulum imagine that it's some kind of perpetual motion machine that keeps going on and on by itself. But the pendulum has a secret— a small electromagnet, high up where it can't be seen, which keeps the pendulum swinging. Even so, from time to time, if the power fluctuates or the building vibrates, the even swing of the pendulum can be interrupted. Then a human starter, wearing white gloves to keep the brass shiny, pulls the bob out beyond the line of pegs, lines it up exactly so that it will swing across the center of the circle—and lets it go.

Far left: Workers on a scaffold clean and repair the Star-Spangled Banner in 1982.

Left: The Foucault Pendulum in motion.

67

A New Look at the First Ladies

"The more I bear, the more is expected," sighed Louisa Adams, wife of the sixth president of the United States, ". . . and I sink in the efforts I make to answer such expectations." But she only had to deal with her husband's political friends and enemies. Some seventy-five years later, first lady Edith Roosevelt had to cope with the press and photographers: "One hates to feel that all one's life is public property," she said. For recent first ladies, it has been impossible to escape constant media attention.

The exhibition First Ladies: Political Role and Public Image, which re-opened in 1992, shows the difficulties—but also the triumphs—that go with the role of first lady. Many presidents' wives have seen it as a chance to take part in American public life, whether campaigning for their husbands or advancing their own causes. Through pictures, diaries, clothing, posters, and many other fascinating things, you can see how life for American women has changed in the last two hundred years—and how first ladies have played a role in those changes.

As far back as the eighteenth century, Abigail Adams reminded her husband—one of the drafters of the Declaration of Independence—that women wanted political rights, too. Now, at the end of the twentieth century, Hillary Rodham Clinton makes no apologies for playing a powerful public role. Someday, when a woman is president, will her husband be "first man"? What do you think will be expected of him?

Top: Mamie Eisenhower and Pat Nixon, the wives of the 1952 and 1956 Republican candidates, became famous themselves as they helped their husbands' campaigns.

Middle: Hillary Clinton on a state visit to Japan. The welfare of children has been one of her key interests as first lady.

Bottom: During her years in the White House, Barbara Bush visited many schools as part of her literacy campaign.

FIRST LADY FIRSTS

◆ **First to be criticized for having too much influence over presidential policies: Abigail Adams (1797-1801)**
Political foes of President John Adams mockingly referred to her as "Mrs. President."

◆ **First to live in the White House: Abigail Adams**
The Executive Mansion was an unfinished and uncomfortable home when Abigail lived there. She hung her laundry in what would become the East Room.

◆ **First to be called "first lady": Mary Todd Lincoln (1861-1865)**
A couple of years earlier, Harriet Lane, niece and hostess for unmarried President James Buchanan, had been called "first lady" in a magazine story.

◆ **First to graduate from college: Lucy Hayes (1877-1881)**
Lucy graduated from Cincinnati's Wesleyan Female College in 1850.

◆ **First to be married in the White House: Frances Cleveland (1886-1889 and 1893-1897)**
President Grover Cleveland was 27 years older than his bride. She became, at age 21, the youngest first lady in U.S. history.

◆ **First to have her own secretary: Edith Roosevelt (1901-1909)**
There was enormous interest in the large and energetic Roosevelt family (six children and a host of pets). Edith hired a social secretary to deal with demands for stories and pictures of the family.

◆ **First to make a radio broadcast from the White House: Lou Hoover (1929-1933)**
As the Great Depression began, she made broadcasts urging American women to donate food and clothing for the needy.

◆ **First to hold weekly press conferences: Eleanor Roosevelt (1933-1945)**
During the 1930s, she held her own weekly press conferences, open only to female journalists.

FIRST LADY OF THE WORLD

In 1933, her first year in the White House, first lady Eleanor Roosevelt traveled 38,000 miles making inspection trips across the country. The next year, she traveled 42,000 miles. After that, she made so many appearances that newspapers gave up trying to keep track of her mileage! Because President Franklin Delano Roosevelt had been partly paralyzed by polio and couldn't move around easily, she was determined to report back to him on conditions all over the United States.

Those were hard years, when many Americans were without jobs, housing, or even enough food to eat. Mrs. Roosevelt could be counted on to support any program that would improve life for underprivileged people. She believed passionately in human rights for all Americans, and wasn't afraid to speak out. For instance, when a women's organization would not allow the great black singer Marian Anderson to give a concert in a Washington audito-

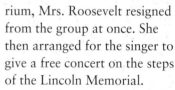

rium, Mrs. Roosevelt resigned from the group at once. She then arranged for the singer to give a free concert on the steps of the Lincoln Memorial.

While her husband served three terms as president, including the difficult years of World War II, Eleanor kept up her compassionate work. She made speeches, and wrote newspaper columns and magazine articles, becoming the most admired woman in the country.

After her husband died in 1940, the new president, Harry Truman, appointed her a U.S. delegate to the United Nations. Now she had truly become, as President Truman called her, "First Lady of the World."

DRESS DETECTIVES, STITCH BY STITCH

Since the First Ladies Collection was begun in 1912, millions of people have gazed with delight at the first ladies' gowns. But all the years the delicate dresses were on display, they were being weakened by dust, light, and changing temperatures.

In 1987, the First Ladies Hall was closed for renovations and conservation work. In the two years that the exhibit was closed, curators and conservators became dress detectives, making the most detailed study of the dresses that had ever been done.

They went over the fabric and stitches inch by inch and even looked at the fibers under microscopes. At the same time, they gathered all the information they could about when each dress had been made, how it had originally looked, and how it

had changed over the years. They looked at portraits, read newspaper descriptions of the clothes, and tracked down the historical records of dressmakers whose labels they found inside the dresses.

Lucretia Garfield's 1881

inaugural gown, for example, appears to be an off-white color. Yet an 1881 newspaper story about the event describes the dress as lavender. What had happened to change it? When the dress fabric was chemically analyzed, conservators found that it had been dyed with fuschine, a nineteenth-century dye extremely sensitive to light. Over the years, the dress had faded to its present pale shade. However, color readings taken with an instrument called a *spectrocolorimeter* from un-faded areas inside the dress revealed its original color. Now, when the dress is displayed, a color-corrected photo is placed beside it.

An Unsolved Mystery

One of the most fragile dresses in the collection is the wedding dress of Sarah Yorke Jackson, who married President Andrew Jackson's adopted son in 1831 and served as presidential hostess. Careful study uncovered the many changes the dress had undergone, as several generations of women in the family wore it. It is clear, for instance, that the bodice and underskirt of the dress were not part of it in 1831. The words "Skinner's Satin" are woven into the edge of the fabric, and this company did not begin making satin until the late 1870s.

However, the style of the dress bodice is a remaining puzzle for the Smithsonian's curators. Its pointed waist, laced back and other details point to the 1860s—but that is too early for the satin. Sarah Yorke Jackson's daughter, who donated the dress to the Smithsonian in 1922, told curators that she had remade the dress's bodice in order to make it look as it should have. Did she use the Skinner's satin to copy a bodice that had been worn with the dress in about 1860, and which she mistook for the original?

While this puzzle may never be solved, the conservators did solve the problem of how to save the silk chiffon of the original 1831 dress. Tiny fragments of fabric were test cleaned with different chemicals and then examined under the microscope to see which worked best. The chemical treatment that was chosen not only made the dress cleaner, but softened the starch that had made it brittle. The dress can now be displayed in a special low-light case, where it lies flat to prevent further damage.

Dresses worn by twentieth-century first ladies: from left to right, Edith Roosevelt, Edith Wilson, Helen Taft, Mamie Eisenhower, Florence Harding, Lou Hoover, Eleanor Roosevelt, Jacqueline Kennedy, and Nancy Reagan.

EVERYDAY LIFE-200 YEARS AGO!

The exhibition After the Revolution tells about the lives of ordinary people—farmers, craftsmen, shop owners, merchants, and slaves—who lived in the area occupied by the original thirteen states during the last twenty years of the eighteenth century. Here you'll get to know farm and plantation families; city-dwellers; and Native Americans and African Americans, both slave and free.

MEET THE SPRINGERS

The first people you'll meet are a Delaware farm family named the Springers: Elizabeth, the mother; Thomas, the father; and two young daughters, Mary and Anne. In fact, not only will you meet the Springers, you'll get to walk right through the middle of their house! It's a two-story log house with two rooms, one upstairs and one down. The part you'll see is the big downstairs room, where the family gathered around the fireplace, ate their meals, and did their chores, and where the father and mother slept.

The girls slept upstairs in a room also used for storage. Cooking was done outdoors, in a lean-to shed. There was no running water for baths or doing dishes; water had to be carried from a well. An outdoor shed contained a toilet—just a hole in the ground with a wooden seat. The only heat in the house came from the fireplace. Candles and oil lamps provided light.

Even though it may look bare to you, the Springer house was better furnished than most other farmhouses in the area. Whitewashed walls, a china tea set, and other small luxuries tell us that a relatively well-off family lived here. But something is missing . . . where are the children's toys?

In the Springer household, as in most farm households of the time, there were no toys, or very few. Children had little time for toys because they were so busy helping their parents. Boys did field chores like plowing, chopping wood, and digging ditches, while girls spun, wove, knitted, cleaned, cooked, milked the cows, and helped to bring in the crops during the harvest. From dawn to dusk, children worked alongside their parents and any servants or slaves the family might have. Even younger children had jobs to do, like shucking corn, shelling peas, and weeding the garden. The Springer household was unusual because it had only two children; most families had more.

With all that work, there was little time for kids to go to school. What little schooling most farm children received, they got at home. As the family sat around the fire on winter evenings, parents taught reading, writing, and arithmetic. In addition, girls were taught to sew, often by embroidering "samplers." By working alongside their parents, children learned the practical skills they would need as adults.

But although children worked hard, they still managed to have fun. They enjoyed songs and stories and being out-of-doors. They made friends with children from neighboring farms. While tending the animals, they took time out to pet the young ones.

You can find out more about the Springers in the Hands on History Room (see pp. 78-79). Look for a trunk filled with unusual stuff that the Springers used every day.

City Life, 1790

An engraving of a Philadelphia street scene in the 1790s.

Did you know that in 1790, 95 percent of the people in the United States lived on farms or in villages? Only 5 percent were city dwellers (compared to 65 percent today).

The major cities of the time were Boston, New York, and Philadelphia, but Philadelphia was the biggest and the most important, with 42,000 people.

Making your way along its narrow, bustling streets, you'd meet wealthy merchants, poor slaves and servants, shop girls and shop owners, sailors, doctors and lawyers, construction workers, seamstresses, housewives and craftspeople.

Along the riverfront, tall-masted ships lay docked. Some were unloading goods from foreign ports, such as sugar, molasses, and tea. Others were taking on American products, such as grain, timber, and livestock, to sell overseas.

Dozens of small shops lined the streets. Many were owned by craftspeople or "artisans," who made by hand the goods that people needed. Each one specialized in a particular product, such as shoes, furniture, or bread. Many young people aspired to learn a craft, because artisans were prosperous and well-respected. The first step to realizing this ambition was to become an apprentice.

Around the age of fourteen you would move in with the family of an artisan whose craft you wanted to learn. For seven years, you would work long hours without pay. In return, the artisan would provide food, clothing, lodging, and training in the craft. He would also teach you to read and write.

If all went well, at age twenty-one you would be given a certificate saying that you had learned the skills necessary to become a "journeyman." The artisan might also give you a new outfit of clothes, called a "freedom suit." Armed with your certificate, and dressed in your new suit, you could hire yourself out to work for pay in the shops of other artisans. Then you could start saving money so that one day you could go into business for yourself.

AMAZING BUT TRUE
THE RAID ON SAMUEL COLTON

Another part of After the Revolution takes you to the village of Longmeadow, Massachusetts, where you'll meet Samuel Colton, a wealthy merchant. You can participate in a trial just as it took place in 1781. Here's the story:

Five years earlier, during the Revolutionary War, Colton's neighbors raided his store because they thought his prices were unfair. Under the cover of night, they took his goods, and sold them for what they thought were fair prices. Then they returned the money to Colton.

After the war was over, Colton took his neighbors to court, charging robbery. They argued, in defense, that since they had returned the money, it was not robbery; they had merely been acting for the good of the community. During the Revolution, the courts of law were temporarily out of business, so they claimed it was alright for them to take justice into their own hands. In the end, the court agreed with them and found them not guilty. What do you think? Were Samuel Colton's neighbors guilty? Do you think a court would reach the same verdict if a similar incident happened today?

MEET THE CORN GROWERS

In another part of After the Revolution, you can learn what life was like for the Seneca nation of the Iroquois Confederacy. In the 1790s, they had settlements in New York, Ohio, and Canada. Like many other groups of American Indians, the Seneca struggled to survive as Europeans took over their lands and killed the animals they needed for food and clothing.

One thing that did not change for the Seneca during this period, however, was corn. For generations, corn had been their most important crop The Indians introduced corn to the Europeans, who had never seen it before. The newcomers quickly took a liking to it and started to grow it, too. If it hadn't been for corn, many of the European newcomers would have starved to death. Today corn is still one of the most important crops grown in North America.

SLAVE LIFE IN THE CHESAPEAKE

Another stop in After the Revolution is the Chesapeake region of Virginia, where tobacco and wheat were grown. African Americans, most of them slaves, made up almost half the population here in 1790. A landowner could make a lot of money growing tobacco; however, his success depended on hard manual labor. Slaves, captured and brought from Africa, supplied this labor. In addition to working in the fields, slaves also worked as household servants.

Living conditions among the slaves of the Chesapeake varied a lot. Field hands probably suffered the most, often living in ramshackle quarters with meager food and no privacy. House servants were generally treated better. None of the slaves, however, no matter how "fortunate," had any personal freedom. They had no money, no property, no education, and no right to choose where they wanted to live or with whom.

In After the Revolution, you can see old posters and other drawings of slaves in the Chesapeake. You'll also see some of the household items and tools that slaves used daily. Because few such items still exist, and there are few written records, historians have a less complete picture of the slaves' daily lives than those of their white owners.

Above: Uncovering a pewter spoon in the Mount Vernon slave quarters.

Another record of slave life at Mount Vernon is this 1796 portrait, by Edward Savage, of George Washington's family. The man at far right is William Lee. Lee was Washington's slave and personal servant. He accompanied Washington in his battles during the Revolutionary War—and everywhere else the general traveled in later life. When Washington died, his will gave Lee his freedom, in gratitude for his service.

AMAZING BUT TRUE

AFRICAN AMERICAN SLAVES AT MOUNT VERNON

As you probably know, Mount Vernon was the farm of George Washington, our first president. What you may not know is that George Washington and his wife, Martha, owned many slaves. Recently, archaeologists started excavating the slave quarters at Mount Vernon to learn more about how these African Americans lived. Here's what they found and what their discoveries tell us:

◆ Buckles and cufflinks: give an idea of how the slaves at Mount Vernon decorated their clothing

◆ Bones of chicken, fish, and small mammals; seeds of various kinds: give an idea of what they ate

◆ Pieces of pottery: show what kind of dishes slaves used

◆ Gun shot: suggests that they hunted for some of their food

◆ Marbles: show that the Mount Vernon slaves sometimes played at least one game—and maybe others.

Mount Vernon today.

GET YOUR HANDS ON HISTORY

The big, bright Hands on History room is designed especially for kids and their families. More than thirty activities offer a chance for everyone to learn about history by **doing.** Nearly every subject in the museum is touched on here, so a visit to Hands on History will make your museum experience complete. Here are some of the activities that await you:

◆ For *Little House on the Prairie* fans, get a taste of what living in a sod house was like for pioneer children and their families. Look at old photographs, read about daily life, and explore a trunk filled with things used by sod house dwellers.

◆ Take White's Efficiency Test to see if you're dexterous enough to be a postal clerk on the railroad in 1870.

◆ Walk the roads of upstate New York with an immigrant peddlar in 1848. Meet the people he met and poke through his pack to find out what he sold.

◆ Unpack the trunk of Betsy, a little girl from a Virginia plantation, to find clues about a child's life in the 1780s.

Study the designs on Zuni and Santa Clara pots. Discover what the symbols mean, and decorate a paper pot with symbols of your own.

◆ Or try your hand at ginning cotton, harnessing a mule, making rope, sending a telegram, using a treadle sewing machine, or riding a high-wheel bicycle—all in one place!

Hands on History is open from noon to 3 p.m., Tuesday through Sunday. Tickets are required during busy times. They are free, and may be picked up on a first-come, first-served basis at the door of the room.

ASK THE EXPERTS ◆ ◆ ◆
HOW TO RIDE A HIGH-WHEEL BICYCLE

How do I climb on board?
Stand with your feet on either side of the small rear wheel and hold the handle grips. With your right foot, step onto a step stool. Put the toe of your left foot on the small step located above the bicycle's rear wheel. Push off with your right foot, raising your right leg, and ease onto the seat. When you pedal, be sure to use the balls of your feet instead of the insteps.

Help! How do I get down?
Return to the step stool and stop in front of it. Place your left toe on the small step located just above the rear wheel. Still holding onto the handle bars, lift yourself off the seat, and drop your right foot onto the step stool. Step back, away from the high-wheeler. You've successfully completed your ride!

BEHIND THE SCENES
A COTTON TALE

Keeping Hands on History up and running is a never-ending job, says Nancy McCoy, the museum's Director of Education.

McCoy is the person in charge of Hands on History. She oversaw its development until it opened a few years ago. And now, with the help of Heather Paisley-Jones, the room's exhibition manager, she makes sure the room is maintained so that visitors will have a good time. This means getting things fixed right away when they break. It also means keeping supplies on hand—like cotton for the cotton gin.

The cotton gin is one of the most popular things in the room. You put in a handful of cotton and turn the handle. Then you watch in amazement as the teeth of a circular saw separate the small black seeds from the fluffy white fibers (called "lint"). The seeds are spit into a metal cup attached to the front of the gin, while the lint is pushed by revolving brushes into a wire cage (called a condenser) in back. Because the gin is so popular with visitors, the museum's supply of cotton is continually being used up.

"Keeping cotton on hand is a lot more complicated than you might think," McCoy told us. "Cotton, as you probably know, comes from a plant that is grown in the South and Southwest. After being picked by machine, our cotton is shipped to the museum by truck."

"Because the museum's storage space is limited, we can only order one bale (a rectangular bundle) of cotton at a time," explained Paisley-Jones. "Each bale costs us about $800 by the time we get it here—and that's not the end of it. Handling it once it arrives at the museum's loading dock is another story."

Despite its modest dimensions (about the size of a suitcase), a bale of cotton isn't exactly easy to lug around. During baling, the cotton fibers are very tightly packed together, which means that a single bale is extremely heavy—weighing close to 500 pounds!

Upon its arrival at the loading dock, the bale is taken directly to an underground parking area, where its bindings are cut and its pa-

A model of Eli
Whitney's cotton gin,
1792.

per wrapping is removed so that the fibers can begin to loosen up. The next day, museum workers pull the bale apart and stuff the cotton into twenty-five to thirty large trash bags.

Then it's off to a food processing plant for freezing. Yes, freezing! This is to kill any insect pests that might be living among the fibers. After freezing, the cotton is transported back to the museum and stored in a closet behind Hands on History. Then it's brought out for ginning, one basketful at a time. About twelve months later, it will be time to order another bale.

A Journey of Hope

LABORERS WANTED 35¢ AN HOUR $3.85 A DAY HIGHER WAGES

If you've ever moved to a strange new place, you know that it takes a while to get used to a new home, to find your way around, and to make some friends. And you'll understand something about the feelings of African Americans—hundreds of thousands of them—who made a brave and hopeful journey from the South to the North between 1915 and 1940. We call this movement of people from southern farms to northern cities the Great Migration.

In the rural South in those days, many African American families made their living growing cotton. Few owned their own land; instead they were sharecroppers, or tenant farmers, who worked the land of white landlords. Each year, they kept only a small portion of the income that came from the cotton they had raised.

Left: Migrant workers in North Carolina head north to seek work.

Above: A woman and boy on their way from North Carolina to New Jersey, where they would pick potatoes. It was July, 1940, and, like many migrants, they took only what they could pack in a suitcase or tie to their car.

The rest of the money went to their landlords. Despite working very hard, these families had barely enough to live on.

Even worse than being poor was the lack of basic human rights. Special laws kept many blacks from voting, and opportunities for schooling were limited by laws prohibiting black children from attending the same schools as white children. Moreover, blacks couldn't move about freely or sit where they pleased in public places. In restaurants, movie theaters, and on buses and trains, they had to stay in special sections apart from whites. If they went where they weren't supposed to go, either accidentally or on purpose, they could be thrown in jail or even killed. Cross burnings, lynchings, and other acts of violence against African Americans, by groups like the Ku Klux Klan, were terrifyingly frequent.

In the Field to Factory exhibition, you can meet a girl of about ten named Naomi, whose mother and father were sharecroppers. At the beginning of the exhibition, you'll see Naomi and her parents working together in the cotton fields. It is spring, and they are hoeing the rows of young plants. Earlier in the year, Naomi's father turned up the earth with a mule-drawn plow and planted the cotton seeds. Then the seeds sprouted. Now the young plants need constant weeding and thinning to ensure a good crop. In the fall, the cotton will be hand picked and taken to a nearby cotton gin. Growing and harvesting cotton in this way—without the help of machinery—was extremely hard work. The entire family had to help.

The house that Naomi's family lived in was typical of sharecroppers' houses of that time. There was one big main room, where the family cooked and ate their meals, did chores, listened to a squeaky old phonograph, and sat around and talked. In Field to Factory you can see this room, with its iron stove (used for both cooking and heat), unpainted walls, and plain wooden furniture. A bright homemade quilt, pictures on the wall, and Naomi's rag doll sitting on a chair by the stove help to give the room a cozy feeling.

Like most other sharecroppers, Naomi's family did not own their house but rented it from the landlord. Because their house was so small, the family spent a lot of their time on the front porch or in the

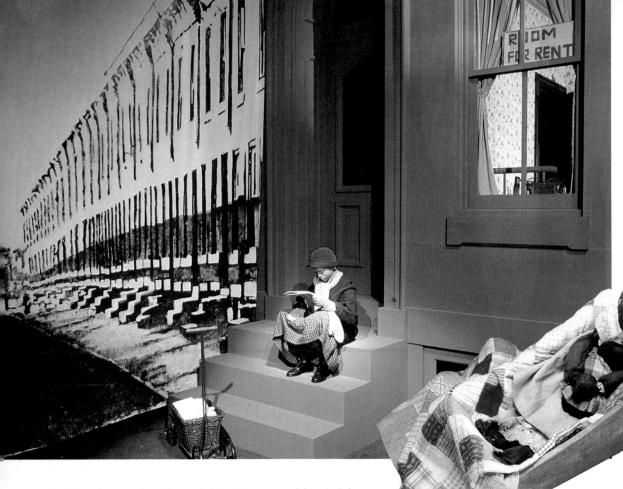

Although in some ways life up North was better, adjusting to a new place was certainly not easy. When she got to the city, Naomi started school right away and soon learned to read and write. Her father was working in a factory now—and her mother was taking in laundry. After school, Naomi would help out by delivering the clean laundry in her wagon. Although the family was still poor, they had more money than they did when they lived in the South. In fact, Naomi even had her own bedroom, which you can see in Field to Factory. She also got her own pair of roller skates—the old-fashioned kind that you clamped onto the bottoms of your shoes and tightened with a key worn on a string around your neck. She was a city girl now, and life was filled with busy schedules and exciting new possibilities.

yard when the weather allowed. The closeness of family life helped to provide a cushion against the poverty and unfair treatment that nearly all southern African Americans suffered in those days.

In the meantime, up North, families could hope for higher wages and a better education for their children as well as the right to vote and even to run for office. Still, it was hard to give up the strong ties of family and friendship. And it was also hard to raise money for the journey. Many families went in stages: a mother or father would go first, get a job, and then save enough money to send for other family members. Field to Factory shows Naomi traveling North all by herself, to join her mother and father. Like many other children who made the trip by train then, she has a note pinned to her coat for the conductor, telling her name and where she is going. She also has her doll and a quilt from home to keep her company.

Life in the North offered many more opportunities for Naomi and her family. Sometimes, though, she missed the fragrant summer mornings and her grandparents down South.

SPENCER CREW AND THE STORY BEHIND FIELD TO FACTORY

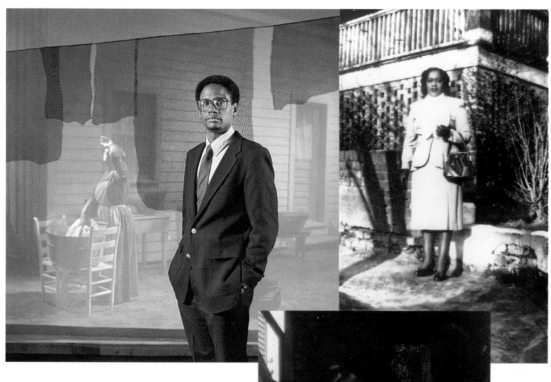

Another reason Mr. Crew chose this topic was that the Great Migration happened within living memory: "There were many people still alive who had actually participated in the migration. We knew we could go to those people to get much of the information we needed, as well as objects to use in the show."

While gathering materials, Spencer Crew was surprised to find out a lot he hadn't known about his own family. Spencer Crew was born and raised in the North and now lives near Washington, D.C., but he learned that his grandfather, Rufus Crew (shown below left, with an unidentified relative), had come from rural South Carolina. His grandfather moved first to Atlanta, Georgia, and later to Cleveland, Ohio. Spencer Crew's father, R. Spencer Crew, was just two years old when his family moved to Cleveland. Lois Crew, R. Spencer's sister, was a teenager. She first took a job as a domestic servant while attending night school. With the money she saved from her salary, she went to college and earned a teaching certificate. Then she got a job teaching in the Cleveland public schools. (Teaching was one of the few professions open to African American women back then.)

Spencer Crew (above), historian and Director of the American History Museum, created the Field to Factory exhibition with a team that included a designer, a writer, and a person from the museum's education department. "Although Field to Factory is about African Americans in particular," Mr. Crew recently explained, "it is also a story to which nearly everyone can feel a strong personal connection. In the United States, almost every family's history involves ancestors who at one time or another moved to a new place to build a better life."

Above right: Another of Spencer Crew's aunts also took part in the Great Migration. To fulfill her dream of becoming a nurse, Lillian Reuben-McNeary left South Carolina in 1940 and moved to New York City.

FROM WOOD TO PLASTIC, FROM LINEN TO LYCRA

If you happen to enter the American History museum by the Constitution Avenue entrance on the first floor, you can start your visit with the Material World exhibit. Since it deals with what everyday things are made of, and why, it makes a great introduction to the museum as a whole.

Your bedroom and the things in it are very different from the room your grandmother or grandfather grew up in. Your toys are different. The clothes hanging in your closet are different too. One big reason for these differences is the materials from which your belongings are made. When your grandparents were children, toys were made of metal, cloth, rubber, wood, and an early, brittle form of plastic called "celluloid." There was nothing like the brightly colored, soft, bendable plastic toys you have today. All the synthetic materials that can make clothes drip-dry, permanent press, waterproof, and windproof—as well as stretchy, shiny and even glow-in-the-dark—hadn't been invented yet.

All around your house are things that weren't in your grandparents' houses. They probably had radios—in wooden cabinets. But almost nobody had a TV set. There were no computers and no video games. In fact, these things couldn't even be invented until the things they were made of—like silicon chips and moldable plastics—had been invented.

Still, your grandparents lived in a wonderful world of conveniences and entertainments—indoor plumbing, trains, planes, movies—compared with Americans of some two hundred years ago. In the 1700s, most people lived on farms, grew or raised their own food, and made all their own household goods from natural materials like clay, wood, linen, wool, iron, copper, and tin. In the next century, American industry began to grow, and many rural people moved into the cities to work in factories. Machine-made objects began to replace things made at home by hand. In the 1850s, new ways were found to change iron into steel. Steel—stronger and easier to shape than iron—transformed the look of America. Soon it was being used in all kinds of products, from food cans to road signs to railroad ties to bicycle wheels. And it was steel's superior strength, when used in beams and girders, that made possible a new kind of building—the skyscraper!

Many other important new materials came along around the same time as steel, and now they're so much a part of our everyday lives that it's hard to imagine what we did without them:

◆ Aluminum—strong, rust-resistant, and lightweight—was at first so expensive to produce that it was used only for luxury items like opera glasses and ladies' fans. However, a new way of processing aluminum, discovered in the 1880s, made it cheap enough to use on big commercial products. In the twentieth century it became the material of choice for airplanes and spacecraft, as well as for such everyday things as cooking pots and household siding.

◆ Rubber was first manufactured in 1839 by treating the sticky sap of a tropical tree by a process called *vulcanization*. It was found to be ideal for things like waterproof gloves and raincoats, balls, and bicycle tires. Today, rubber still gets lots of use; however, it is no longer manufactured from tree sap but is made synthetically.

◆ Glass is an ancient material made from sand. Industry started mass-producing it in the late nineteenth century for use in new products like light bulbs and milk bottles. Later, in the twentieth century, a special kind of glass was invented to withstand heat, making glass cookware possible. Around the same time, fiberglass—used for products ranging from draperies to surfboards—was invented.

Today the materials we have to work with to create new products are enormously varied, and new ones are being developed all the time. Each of these "synthetics" has its own special properties, like being tough and fire-proof . . . or soft and warm . . . or easy to clean. Advances in modern chemistry are responsible for an explosion in new product development.

Opposite: Table radios and American Beauty iron from the 1930s; 1940s Maytag washing machine; and 1950s Mix-o-matic mixer.

Right: 1946 AMI Model A jukebox.

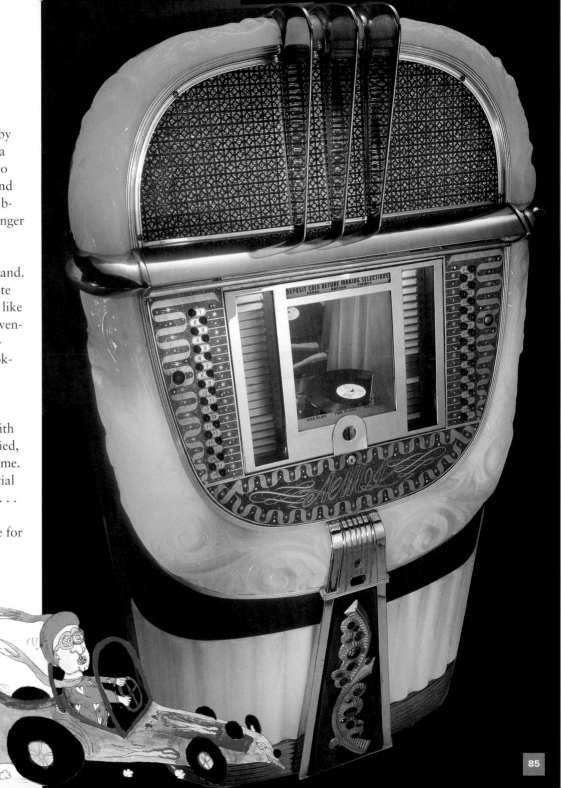

Don't Miss It!

Off to your left as you enter the museum from Constitution Avenue is a real country store post office, which looks, feels, and even smells old! It was built in 1860 and brought to the museum in 1971, along with its stove, furnishings, and much of its merchandise. You can walk inside, buy stamps, mail letters to your friends, and just enjoy browsing around. Any letters you mail will be canceled with a special "Smithsonian Station" postmark.

The Swamp Rat XXX

One of the most amazing objects in Material World is a low, sleek vehicle with a pointy nose, called the Swamp Rat XXX. This dragster, built by top racer "Big Daddy" Don Garlits, can travel faster than 435 kilometers (270 miles) per hour. One secret of the Swamp Rat's success is the durable, lightweight materials from which it is made. In fact, there are more than twenty different materials—with names like Kevlar, Nomex, and chromium molybdenum alloy steel—in the Swamp Rat's body, wheels, and engine. Each one has a particular purpose, from retarding fire in case of a crash to providing super strength and flexibility.

The streamlined cockpit is modeled on aircraft design. The frame, which is similar to bicycle and airplane frames, weighs only 93.9 kilograms (250 pounds). In fact, the entire Swamp Rat weighs only 681 kilograms (1825 pounds).

GIANT CABLES

The George Washington Bridge spans the Hudson River, linking Manhattan Island with New Jersey. The bridge is hung from giant cables exactly like the one shown in the Material World exhibit. Each cable is made from 26,474 steel wires squeezed tightly together. Each separate wire is strong enough to support a weight of more than 7,000 pounds—equal to one adult elephant! Together, the four cables can hold 184 million tons of cars, trucks, buses, and people! The George Washington Bridge was built back in 1931, and people have been relying on it ever since to get across the Hudson River safely.

ALL ABOARD!

In the mid-1800s, the United States was growing fast. Cities and factories were booming. Thousands of people were moving West. And at the heart of all this commotion—was locomotion!

In the Railroad hall, a passenger car from the Camden and Amboy Railway in New Jersey shows you what travel was like in the 1830s. The car is much smaller than modern passenger cars. The narrow wooden seats, with no springs, are upholstered in velvet, and the windows slide open. You could get fresh air—but you'd also get dust in your eyes, and soot from the engine! Because of the crude way the cars were coupled (with a simple link and pin system), you could count on their bumping together as the train speeded up and slowed down. If you didn't hold on tight, you'd go sprawling!

The Final Spike

Right after the Civil War, the building of the transcontinental railroad began. The United States government contracted with two railroad companies—the Union Pacific and the Central Pacific—to complete this enormous task. The Union Pacific started in Omaha, Nebraska (where already existing track from the East Coast ended), and built westward, while the Central Pacific started in Sacramento, California, and built eastward. It was one of the most ambitious engineering projects ever, taking six-and-a-half years to lay 2857 kilometers (1775 miles) of track.

Far left: The *1401* came to the museum in 1961. An entire wall of the museum had to be removed to let it in, and the floor on which it is resting had to be reinforced to support its 188 1/2 tons. When it was in service, with its load of coal and water, it weighed 280 tons!

Left: The Union Pacific Railroad flooded the country with posters like this after the linkup of the trans-continental railroad in 1869.

Chinese and Irish immigrants, African Americans, and Civil War veterans from both North and South, wielding pick axes, shovels, and hammers, did most of the work. On May 10, 1869, at Promontory Point, Utah, the two crews finally joined up and laid the final stretch of track. Telegraph wires signalled "Done!" from coast to coast, and the entire country celebrated.

A Whole New Era

The railroad made it possible for many people to go places they'd never been before. Now a trip all the way from New York to San Francisco took just eight to ten days. And since railroad cars had been improved considerably—with springy seats and plenty of leg room—the trip could be made in comfort.

The era of the steam locomotive lasted for more than one hundred years, right up until the early 1950s. All that time, locomotive builders kept improving on the design of the engines, making them bigger, more powerful, and more efficient. Some steam engines built between 1925 and 1950 could pull up to 100 freight cars (or up to 20 passenger cars) at speeds of more than 129 kilometers (80 miles) per hour!

One of these later locomotives was the *1401*, on display in the Railroad hall. Coal stored in the tender car (behind the engine) was used to heat water. This produced steam, powering the locomotive.

Yet even during the *1401*'s later glory days, steam locomotives were on their way out. Locomotives burning diesel fuel—cleaner and cheaper to operate—became more popular in the 1940s. By the 1960s, they had replaced steam engines altogether.

Still sleek, silvery diesel engines have never had the romance of the old steam engines. To many people who remember the old days, they just don't sound right. Hang around for a while near the *1401*, and sure enough, you'll hear it—the engine starts up with a powerful chug-a-chug-a-chug-a-chug, and the whistle lets out a piercing blast—whoo-awhoo! It's easy to imagine pulling out of the station after the conductor calls, "All aboard!"

THE ONE AND ONLY JOHN BULL

Of all the objects in its railroad collection, the one of which the museum is most proud is an old steam locomotive called the *John Bull*. It's on display outside the Railroad hall.

Like many of the early locomotives used in the United States, the *John Bull* was made in England. It was built in 1831 for an American railroad company, and it had a top speed of 64 kilometers (40 miles) per hour. Although this doesn't seem like much of a thrill today, it was about four times as fast as most people in those days had ever gone!

The *John Bull* has belonged to the Smithsonian since 1885. In 1981, to celebrate its 150th birthday, museum workers took it out for a run (shown above). You can see a videotape showing the *John Bull* in action, chugging effortlessly down tracks along the old C&O (Chesapeake and Ohio) Canal. This experiment proved what an important treasure the *John Bull* really is—the oldest self-propelled vehicle in the entire world that can still run!

On the Road

Hurray for the Horseless Carriage!

In the 1890s, the automobile, or "horseless carriage," came rumbling into town—and changed American life forever. The Road Transportation hall houses a wonderful collection of early autos. The first cars were manufactured just a few at a time, which made them very expensive. Soon, however, with mass production, manufacturers could make cars more cheaply, so that more and more people could afford them. Owning their own cars gave Americans an efficient way to do their jobs and transport goods, as well as the freedom to get out and explore their country. By 1917, the automobile was no longer a novelty but a fact of everyday life.

Most of the earliest autos were powered by steam or electricity. The 1894 Balzer has a small, wooden seat and a tubular metal frame. It is named for the man who designed and built it, Stephen Balzer of New York City. In case you're wondering what happened to the steering wheel, this car never had one! Instead, as with many early autos, a metal tiller, resting on the seat, was used for steering.

The Oldsmobile Curved Dash Runabout was the first make of car ever built on an assembly line. Its price tag was so high that only wealthy people could afford to buy it. Nonetheless, it became the first gasoline-powered auto to outsell electric and steam-powered models. In addition to its shiny good looks, customers appreciated its smooth ride and reliability. By 1903, for reasons of efficiency and ease of use, gasoline took over as the main automobile fuel.

Traveling on wagon trails and railroad right-of-ways, and fording streams, the Winton touring car was the first car ever to cross the United States. Its trek from San Francisco to New York City in sixty-three days in 1903 captured the nation's attention, proving that the horseless carriage was here to stay.

A view of the Road Transportation hall. In the foreground, left to right: 1929 Miller racing car, Bruce Larson's funny car dragster, and a 1948 Tucker. Evel Knievel's 1972 motorcycle is suspended above.

A Bike in Every Garage, Including Yours

In the midst of all the shiny carriages and high-powered cars, it's easy to overlook another fun part of Road Transportation: over a century-and-a-half of people- and pedal-powered machines.

The oldest machine in the bicycle collection doesn't have pedals, but it does qualify as the great-grandfather of the modern bicycle. The homely little wooden vehicle called the *draisine* dates from 1818. In order to ride it, you had to straddle the seat and push the ground with your feet. This made for rather slow going—unless, of course, you were coasting downhill. Then WATCH OUT—no brakes!

In the 1860s, a bicycle with pedals called a *velocipede* was introduced (shown at right). When you hopped onto its wooden seat, you were in for a rough ride because this bike had *iron* tires. The frame was also made of iron; the wheels were made of wood. The only nod to comfort was a single spring, placed under the seat—hardly enough to cushion the jolts of unpaved roads. All that iron and the placement of the pedals (on the front wheel) also made the velocipede heavy and hard to steer. No wonder its popularity was short lived!

From 1876 until about 1890, a bike called the *high-wheeler* was the rage among men and boys. A tubular steel frame reduced its weight, and ball bearings on the axle helped to smooth the ride. The high-wheel bicycle was, in fact, the first popular type of mechanical, personal transportation. It cost about the same as a horse—but you didn't have to feed it.

The next big improvement in bicycle design was the chain drive safety bicycle, invented in England in 1885 and soon introduced in the United States. By 1892, bikes with rubber over tires, or "safeties," made bike-riding a much more comfortable—and popular—means of transportation. The production of bicycles exploded fivefold in the ten years between 1889 and 1899, making them affordable for almost everyone. And the love affair with bicycles continues to this day!

Henry Ford's Dream

Henry Ford, seated on an 1896 Quadricycle, one of his early vehicles.

In the late 1800s, a man named Henry Ford from Michigan had a dream: to make a car for everyone.

While other automakers were busy catering to the needs of the wealthy few, Ford saw an opportunity in marketing to everyday people, such as shopkeepers, farmers, and people working in offices.

He dreamed of an automobile so easy to drive that a person with no experience could quickly master the controls. He dreamed of a car that would be easy to fix—and affordable to practically everyone. He dreamed of millions of people driving this car everywhere, and their lives made easier and richer as a result.

Ford's first car, the Model A, was built in his shop in 1903 and sold modestly well. Over the next five years, he continued to experiment with additional models. One thing he needed to create his ideal car was strong but cheap metal for the chassis. He finally found what he was looking for in a steel alloy called vanadium steel. In 1908, he used vanadium steel to create his first Model T.

The Model T, or "Tin Lizzie" as it came to be known, was small, homely, and lightweight, with a folding top, big round headlights, and a top speed of 72 kilometers (45 miles) per hour. It was cheap and reliable, and the American people loved it.

But Ford was still not satisfied. He continued to work on improving his manufacturing methods. His goal was to increase production efficiency of the Model T and lower costs. In 1913, he began using a conveyor belt to move cars along the assembly line—an idea he adapted from the meat packing industry. This saved him a lot of money, and Ford passed the savings on to his customers. Much to everyone's delight, the price of a new Model T actually began to drop—and continued to drop with each passing year! Eventually prices were so low that practically anyone could afford to buy a Ford. By 1927, fifteen million Model Ts had been produced. Henry Ford had made his dream come true.

It's amazing to consider where Ford's dream eventually led us. As automobiles became popular, roads were built and improved all over America. Stores, and then towns, sprang up at crossroads where gas stations had been built. Motoring became one of America's favorite leisure-time activities. For the convenience of vacationing motorists, motels were established along the newly paved roads.

Owing to the genius of Henry Ford, America became a country on wheels. And we remain so to this day.

DREAM ON

You can't miss "Dave's Dream," a sparkling, multicolored work of art near the entrance to the Road Transportation hall. In southern California, Texas, Arizona, and New Mexico, Hispanic people often transform old cars into custom "lowriders." To create these cars, entire families—men and women—work together to modify the frame and suspension to lower the car. They rebuild the engine, rework the body, reupholster the interior, and repaint the outside. These customized beauties are then ready to be exhibited and judged at lowrider shows. "Dave's Dream" was begun by David Jaramillo of New Mexico in 1978. He was killed in a car crash (in a different car) a year later, but his family finished the lowrider in his memory. It won many awards in lowrider shows before it found a home at the Smithsonian.

The interior and exterior of "Dave's Dream."

Information, Please!

Telephones, televisions, radios, and computers. Our lives today depend on these and other "information technologies." That's why the times we live in and this big exhibit are called the "Information Age." The exhibition traces the development of information technologies—and their effect on people's lives—from the mid-1880s until now.

As you enter, be sure to pick up a brochure, with a map of Information Age and its highlights. A barcode, which you can scan at locations in the exhibition marked on the map, allows you to record your visit.

Turn-of-the-Century Telephones

It's hard to imagine life without telephones. How would you ever make plans with your friends, or let your parents know what time you'll be home? Telephones allow us to keep in touch with the people we care about. Oddly, when the telephone was first invented in 1877 by Alexander Graham Bell, it was used only for business. It wasn't until fifteen years later that people started having phones installed in their homes so they could make social calls.

In the beginning, phones had no numbers. Instead, you picked up the phone to get the operator and told her the name of the person you wanted to call. Then she would connect you.

Phone numbers were first used in 1879 in Lowell, Massachusetts, during a measles epidemic. They were introduced to keep the telephone system from breaking down if all the operators became too sick to work.

Many towns had party lines. Your family would share a line with a number of other "parties" (households). Each party was assigned a different sequence of short and long rings. But there was one big problem with this system: everyone else on the party line could eavesdrop on your conversation!

In the early days, operators used plugs on switchboards to connect one phone number with another. In the bigger switch-board stations, where there were several switchboards, the operators had many calls coming in all at once. They had to dash from one switchboard to the next. At first, young boys were hired to do the job because they were quick on their feet. However, since boys often got into mischief, they were later replaced by women. They sometimes wore roller skates to increase the speed at which they could do their jobs!

Above: Two Alexander Graham Bell telephones.

Right: A collection of telephones from the late 19th and early 20th centuries.

Samuel Morse's High-Tech Machine

What do you think of when you think of "high tech?" The latest computer software or video game? The cellular telephone? The information superhighway? Back in the nineteenth century a machine like the telegraph shown at right was on the absolute cutting edge of information technology!

Patented by Samuel Morse in 1840, the telegraph greatly reduced the time it took to send messages. If you lived in Kansas and wanted to let cousins in New Jersey know of the birth of a new baby in your family, you could get the news to them via telegraph in just a few hours. Before the telegraph, it would have taken several days to send your message by mail.

To send a message by telegraph, you went to the nearest telegraph office. An operator keyed in your message on a *transmitter,* and the electrical impulses carrying your message travelled instantaneously over the wires to a telegraph office near your cousins' home. There it was picked up by a *receiver,* which automatically typed or sounded it out in Morse Code. An operator then translated your message back into words and had it delivered by hand.

The telegraph completely changed the way business was done, too. Newspapers—and their readers—could gain access to the news as it happened. Stockbrokers and investors could get up-to-the-minute information about rising and falling prices. Firemen could learn about fires faster, saving more buildings and more lives.

The railroad was one of the first businesses to use the telegraph. Via messages sent up and down the line, stationmasters could keep one another informed about which trains were late and which were on time. This was not only a convenience to passengers. It also helped to reduce the number of accidents caused by trains running into one another on the same track!

A Code Called ENIGMA

You've probably had fun inventing secret codes to send messages to your friends. But did you know that secret codes are not always fun and games? In wartime they're often used to keep information from falling into enemy hands.

During World War II, the Germans used a secret code called ENIGMA for radioing messages among the submarines in their fleet. U.S. ships could pick them up, but technicians in the ships' information centers couldn't decipher their meaning.

Then came the "Bombe," a high-speed calculating machine designed to crack the ENIGMA code. The ability to track German submarines gave the U.S. and its allies a strategic advantage that was key to winning the war. In the exhibition you can learn about cracking the ENIGMA code and see the device the Germans used to send messages in ENIGMA.

You can also see sections of a high-speed information processor called the ENIAC that was developed during World War II. Occupying an entire room when fully assembled, and weighing thirty tons, this machine could solve difficult problems at speeds much faster than ever before possible. People called it the "machine that could think." Like the Bombe, it is considered an important forerunner of the personal computer.

AMAZING BUT TRUE

AND THE WINNER IS . . .

Although computers were invented in the 1940s, the public was only vaguely aware of them until November 6, 1952, when a 16,000-pound computer called UNIVAC I performed an amazing feat, right in people's living rooms. On television screens across the nation, the UNIVAC I correctly predicted the outcome of the presidential elections. It predicted that Republican candidate Dwight D. Eisenhower would win by a landslide over Democrat Adlai E. Stevenson—and he did!

Now we take for granted knowing the outcome of an election ahead of time. But as recently as forty years ago, accurately predicting election results—based on so little information—seemed like a miracle!

A personal computer built from a kit developed by Apple in 1976.

DON'T MISS IT!

Be sure to visit the Videowall Theater in the final section of Information Age for a fifteen-minute multimedia experience exploring the past, present, and future of information technology. And try out the section's many computer interactives to learn first-hand about the role of computers in modern life. For example, you can analyze your own fingerprints just as the FBI would, design a bicycle, direct an automobile plant assembly line, and even redecorate the White House oval office.

It's Not That Easy . . . Finding Me

What is Kermit the frog doing hanging out in Mr. Rogers' neighborhood with a little red-headed marionette from long ago? To find out, stop by one of the most popular exhibitions in American History at the foot of the escalators going from the first floor to the second floor (outside the Information Age exit). Three display cases contain lots of famous objects from radio and television. Some of them—like Kermit or Mr. Rogers' sweater—you will recognize right away from shows you have seen yourself. Others, like the marionette Howdy Doody, are from shows that were on when your parents were kids—or even before they were born. Here are just a few of the many popular items on display:

◆ Props from the television show *M*A*S*H*
◆ A Davy Crockett cap and record
◆ A *Lassie* wallet
◆ Fonzie's leather jacket from *Happy Days*
◆ Archie Bunker's chair from *All in the Family*
◆ Animation cells from *The Flintstones*, *Bugs Bunny,* and *Daffy Duck*
◆ A Mickey Mouse button
◆ Snap, Crackle, and Pop puppets
◆ Superman Radio Quiz Master Game

Everyday Wizardry

Science is so much a part of our daily lives that we often forget it's there. The Science in American Life exhibition looks at how science and scientists have helped shape America's history. By focusing on the debates as well as the advances that scientific discoveries have caused, the exhibition invites you to consider the impact new technologies could have on our future.

This is one of America's first research laboratories. It was established at The Johns Hopkins University in 1876 by a German-trained chemist named Ira Remsen. By founding research laboratories and training young scientists, Remsen had a big influence on the beginnings of scientific research in the United States—especially in chemistry.

Rachel Carson's Early Warning

Growing up on a small Pennsylvania farm in the early 1900s, Rachel Carson developed a love for reading and exploring the outdoors.

These interests eventually led her to become a writer and a scientist. Rachel Carson's first three books made the *New York Times* bestseller list. Her fourth and last book, *Silent Spring,* was an even bigger hit and stirred up enormous controversy.

Until *Silent Spring* came along, most people had assumed that advances in science and technology were unquestionably good. Published in 1962, the book warned Americans of the dangers of certain chemical pesticides. DDT and other chemicals were being sprayed on farmers' fields and suburban lawns to kill mosquitoes and crop-eating insects. Carson showed that birds and other animals were dying out in areas where DDT had been sprayed. She warned that people could get sick and die too.

In her book, Carson argued that all life is interconnected. By poisoning insects, we were also poisoning the birds that ate the insects. Poisons sprayed on our soil eventually ran off into rivers, lakes, streams, and the ocean. By spraying the food we ate, we were poisoning ourselves. Carson didn't argue that we should never use pesticides—only that we should use them carefully.

But many people didn't want to hear Carson's message. The pesticide industry attacked her, as did some scientists. Still her book had been carefully researched and could not be ignored. Today *Silent Spring* is recognized as the work that first made the public aware of the need to protect our environment. Carson's powerful book helped lead to the establishment of the Environmental Protection Agency in 1970, and finally to the ban of DDT in 1972.

Ordinary People, Extraordinary Jobs

Think for a moment about the typical myth of the scientist: Crazy genius. Evil magician. Pale, humorless fellow in white lab coat. These mistaken ideas come mostly from movies, popular fiction, and television. In reality, scientists are ordinary people, with families, friends, and hobbies. Science is the job they do. They do it to earn a living—and because they think it's fascinating. Some work in laboratories, some in offices, and some out-of-doors.

As our scientific knowledge has increased, scientists have become more and more specialized. Trained in particular fields (areas) of science, they work on specific problems. A walk through Science in American Life gives you an idea of how far-ranging the work of scientists really is, from Remsen's pioneering laboratories of the 1800s to an atmospheric chemist studying changes in our ozone layer today.

An Experiment You Could Eat

Popular with kids in the 1920s and 1930s were science sets containing all kinds of stuff for doing experiments. The idea was to encourage children to grow up to be scientists by developing skills that scientists need—like thinking clearly, being patient, and working hard.

Chemistry sets, with their miniature test tubes, beakers, and bunsen burner, brought home some of the excitement of conducting experiments in a real laboratory with real equipment. One popular experiment involved suspending a piece of string in a sugar-water solution. Sugar crystals would form on the string and build on one another to make a piece of rock candy. It was an experiment you could eat!

In the Hands on Science Center in Science in American Life, you can try your hand at removing DNA from a cell, test food for additives, use a Geiger counter to test everyday objects for radioactivity, experiment with methods to clean up an oil spill, and find the ultraviolet rating for your sunglasses.

A typical telegraph set from the 1920s.

Amazing But True
What's New in Biotech?

◆There's a new way to clean up the environment: biotech bugs. These "bugs" are actually micro-organisms—bacteria and fungi—that can eat pollutants and digest them. To get the bacteria to eat faster, scientists feed them a special diet.

◆If you've recently bought a pair of blue jeans with a "well-worn" look, there's a good chance a fungus helped them get that way. This particular kind of fungus secretes an enzyme that can eat denim fibers. The enzyme is collected from the fungus and dumped into a washing machine loaded with blue jeans. Unlike other ways of aging jeans, the fungus method does not pollute the environment.

◆Biotechnologists recently crossed a tomato with an Arctic flounder—really! How did they do it? DNA. DNA is inside the cells of every living thing. It carries the instructions, called genes, that give every plant and animal its own special qualities or "traits." The scientists wanted to give the tomato a particular Arctic flounder trait. That trait was neither the flounder's taste, nor its flatness, nor its swimming skills—but its ability to withstand freezing temperatures. A gene in the flounder's DNA directs its cells to produce a kind of antifreeze that stops ice crystals from forming. So the scientists copied the instructions from the flounder's antifreeze gene and inserted them into the tomato's DNA. Now the tomato has an antifreeze gene, too—and its cells aren't destroyed by freezing temperatures.

FIRST FATHER TO LAST MAN-OF-WAR

The third-floor Armed Forces hall is the home of many artifacts from America's military past. Standouts from the Revolutionary War period include the gunboat *Philadelphia*, the oldest surviving American fighting vessel. You can also see General George Washington's field headquarters tent, and other items belonging to him. Civil War buffs should be sure to see the section devoted to our nation's deadliest conflict.

The Philadelphia's Story

Compared to today's battleships, *Philadelphia* is small and crudely made. Who would guess that this homely vessel played a key role in helping us to win the war against Great Britain?

It was the summer of 1776. British troops were gathering in Canada, planning to take Lake Champlain, in what is now upstate New York, and invade the northern American frontier. Benedict Arnold, leader of a rag tag army of American soldiers, faced the enormous challenge of defending Lake Champlain against an army that was better equipped, more numerous, and better trained.

Working feverishly, Arnold and his men built a fleet of sixteen small wooden vessels, including the *Philadelphia*. When the British invasion began, Arnold stationed his fleet at Valcour Island, near the New York shore of the lake. On October 11, 1776, the two sides met in battle. Although the Americans fought bravely, they couldn't defend themselves against superior British strength and firepower. The *Philadelphia* was hit by a twenty-four-pound cannon ball and sank to the bottom of the lake. There it was to remain for the next 159 years.

In 1781, five years after the *Philadelphia* sank, America won the Revolutionary War. The final victory came at the Battle of Yorktown, in Virginia. But there were other important battles leading up to Yorktown. Proba-

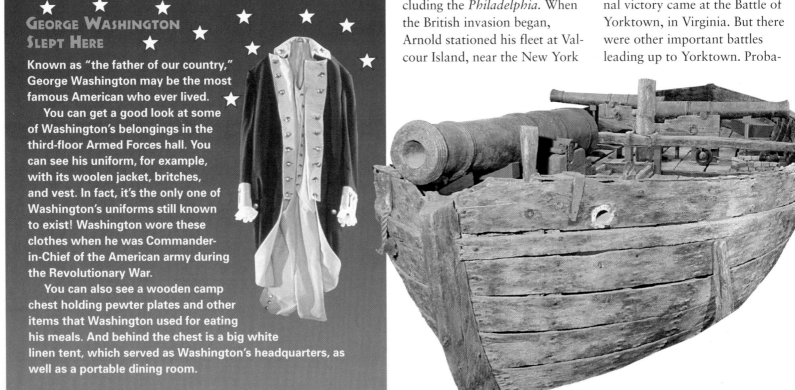

★ ★ ★ GEORGE WASHINGTON SLEPT HERE

Known as "the father of our country," George Washington may be the most famous American who ever lived.

You can get a good look at some of Washington's belongings in the third-floor Armed Forces hall. You can see his uniform, for example, with its woolen jacket, britches, and vest. In fact, it's the only one of Washington's uniforms still known to exist! Washington wore these clothes when he was Commander-in-Chief of the American army during the Revolutionary War.

You can also see a wooden camp chest holding pewter plates and other items that Washington used for eating his meals. And behind the chest is a big white linen tent, which served as Washington's headquarters, as well as a portable dining room.

bly the most critical was the Battle of Saratoga (New York) in 1777. Just one year after his defeat at Valcour Island, Benedict Arnold led a brilliant assault against the British general, John Burgoyne. After long, dark months of defeat, Saratoga gave the Americans new hope and helped convince the French to send troops in support of the American cause.

But what does all of this have to do with the gunboat *Philadelphia?* Well, historians say that if Benedict Arnold's small fleet of wooden boats had not fought so bravely at Valcour, his victory at Saratoga would not have been possible. Even though the British won at Valcour Island, their ships were so badly damaged that they had to delay their battle plans. This gave the American troops time to build up the strength they needed to win at Saratoga. So even though the *Philadelphia* didn't stay afloat for very long, it played a historic role in the Revolutionary War.

In 1935, *Philadelphia* was raised by a salvage engineer with its mainmast still proudly erect—and with many items from 1776 still on board!

How Ruby Slippers and a Doll House Came to the Smithsonian

Some treasures came to the Smithsonian because explorers or scientists went after them—at times even risking their lives to obtain them. Other treasures are purchased for a great deal of money. But many items in American History's collection are gifts given by donors who think that they should be on display for everyone to see.

In some cases, the museum doesn't even know whom to thank. On the third floor you can see one famous example: the chunky, high-heeled shoes that Judy Garland wore as Dorothy in the 1939 movie *The Wizard of Oz*. The red-sequined slippers simply arrived one day, from someone who chose to remain anonymous. They share a display case with a scarecrow costume, a copy of the original book by L. Frank Baum, and a copy of the original movie script, describing Dorothy's special shoes as silver slippers!

The doll house, also on the third floor, was a gift that came directly from its creator. Faith Bradford made or acquired every item in the house, from the little oriental carpets to the tiny goldfish bowls. Mr. and Mrs. Doll and their ten children—along with their servants, visiting grandparents, and pets ranging from a white bulldog to pet rats—all live happily in their twenty-two-room house. Ten children might seem like a large number but this is a family from the early 1900s, when families tended to be bigger than they are now. There's even a photograph of Faith Bradford's cat, Mr. Bittinger, on the wall of the day nursery. And don't forget to take a look in the attic, where the family stores things that are broken or out-of-date.

Even after she gave the doll house to the museum, Faith Bradford still liked to take care of it. Artist's brush in hand, she came to the museum twice a year to clean every one of the Doll family's two thousand possessions. Miss Bradford isn't around any more, but the museum still takes good care of the doll house—and decorates it with wreaths every Christmas.

DON'T MISS IT!

Near the entrance to the Winning the Vote exhibit on the third floor is a dazzling model of the Capitol building. It was made in the early 1970s by Mitsugi Ohno of Manhattan, Kansas, as a Bicentennial project. A wonderful example of the technique known as "lampwork," the model is made of thousands of fused glass rods.

National
Air and Space
Museum

Welcome to the Age of Flight!

National Air and Space Museum
Independence Avenue at 6th Street, SW (shown at left)
Mall entrance: Jefferson Drive at 6th Street, SW

Although we often think of museums as collections of old things, the National Air and Space Museum houses a collection of *new* things. It traces the history of human heavier-than-air flight and space exploration. Hardly anything you'll see here is more than one hundred years old.

1903, the year that Wilbur and Orville Wright first flew a powered airplane, may seem like a very long time ago to you. But there are still a few people alive today who were born before the Wright brothers changed our world by making it possible to fly through the air. And many people—perhaps your great grandparents among them—can remember when an airplane ride was a rare and risky adventure.

The most amazing thing about the Air and Space collection is the technological progress it shows. We've gone from shaky gliders to conducting experiments in outer space—all in the span of one long human lifetime!

As soon as you enter the museum, you will see overhead and all around you famous airplanes and spacecraft. This is the Milestones of Flight gallery, and everything in it represents an important "first," including the Wright brothers' fragile Flyer and the command module that took the Apollo 11 astronauts to the Moon and back. After you've had a good look around, choose one of the exhibit galleries near Milestones of Flight and continue your visit. Each of the galleries on the first and second floors covers a single subject, from Pioneers of Flight to Exploring New Worlds, with lots of fascinating stops in between. Let your imagination soar!

WHERE TO FIND IT

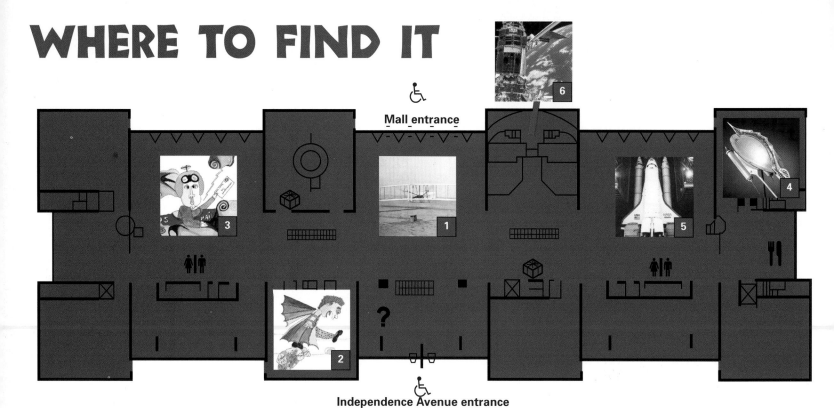

Mall entrance

Independence Avenue entrance

FIRST FLOOR

1 Milestones of Flight
2 Early Flight
3 Air Transportation
4 Rocketry and Space
   Flight
5 Space Hall
6 Samuel P. Langley
   Theater

KEY TO SYMBOLS

? Information
♦ⁱ♦ Restrooms
¶¶ Food service
♿ Accessible entrance
⊠ Elevator
▦ Stairs/Escalator
◇ Museum Shop

Note: Floorplans highlight kid-friendly attractions featured in this book. You can get a complete, up-to-date map at the Information Desk.

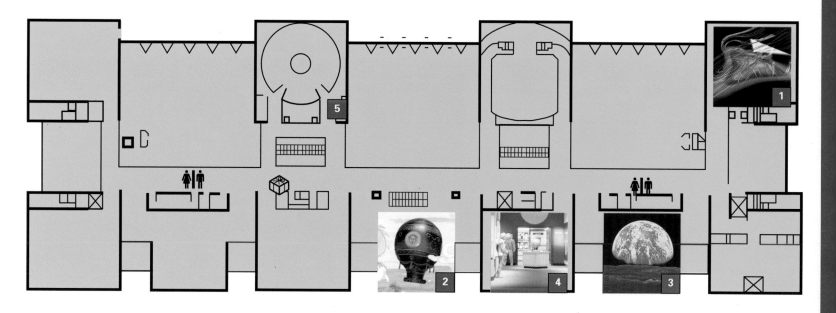

INSIDER TIPS

◆ Guided tours leave daily at 10:15 a.m. and 1 p.m. from the Tour Desk, located just inside the Independence Avenue entrance. Staffed by volunteers, the Tour Desk is also the place where you can have your questions answered and pick up a brochure.

◆ The Langley Theater uses a special projection system called IMAX. IMAX films fill an enormous screen five stories high and seven stories wide. The effect is to give you a realistic feeling of flying through the air or traveling through space. The theater shows four different IMAX films. It's a good idea to get tickets as soon as you arrive at the museum. Admission is $4.00 for adults or $2.75 for those under 21 or over 55.

◆ The Albert Einstein Planetarium offers half-hour programs daily every forty-five minutes beginning at 11:00 a.m. Admission is $4.00 for adults and $2.75 for those under 21 or over 55.

◆ Daily science demonstrations by staff and docents let you explore basic principles of aviation, space flight, and astronomy. Call (202) 357-1400 for information about times, specific subjects, and locations.

THE WRIGHT STUFF

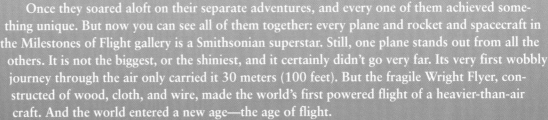

Once they soared aloft on their separate adventures, and every one of them achieved something unique. But now you can see all of them together: every plane and rocket and spacecraft in the Milestones of Flight gallery is a Smithsonian superstar. Still, one plane stands out from all the others. It is not the biggest, or the shiniest, and it certainly didn't go very far. Its very first wobbly journey through the air only carried it 30 meters (100 feet). But the fragile Wright Flyer, constructed of wood, cloth, and wire, made the world's first powered flight of a heavier-than-air craft. And the world entered a new age—the age of flight.

The Flyer was created by two of the world's most famous inventors: Orville and Wilbur Wright. When the Wright brothers were growing up in the Midwest in the 1880s, their father used to travel a lot on business. Sometimes he returned home with presents for his sons. Once he brought them a toy flying machine, powered by tightly wound rubber bands, which provided them with hours of fun.

Later, as grown men, they never gave up their interest in mechanical things, or in flying. In 1899 they wrote to the Smithsonian asking for information on "the proper construction" of such a machine. After reading everything the Smithsonian sent them (including the writings of a man named Otto Lilienthal, which they found especially helpful), they conducted hundreds of experiments on their own.

After much trial and error, on December 17, 1903, the brothers finally did it! From the sand dunes of Kitty Hawk, North Carolina, the Wright Flyer took off on a flight lasting just 12 seconds. From this simple beginning, human beings began to explore the skies, pushing farther and farther away from the earth. And they would never stop, for the whole universe was out there waiting. And to think it all began with a wind-up toy!

Opposite page: Orville (on the left) and Wilbur Wright in their flying clothes.

Top: The Wright Flyer, as it hangs in the Milestones of Flight gallery, "piloted" by a model of Orville Wright.

Bottom: As Wilbur watches, Orville makes history on December 17, 1903— the Flyer rises into the air.

INSPIRED BY THE BIRDS

For hundreds of years before the Wright brothers invented the airplane, people had wanted to fly like birds. Some brave souls even tried to do so, leaping off cliffs or towers with wing-like contraptions attached to their bodies. In the Early Flight gallery (near Milestones of Flight on the first floor), you can find out about one of the most determined of these pioneers, a man whose experiments inspired the Wright brothers.

Otto Lilienthal was the world's first successful glider pilot. He conducted his experiments in the Rhinow hills near his home city of Berlin, Germany. The hills had no trees to get in his way, and the wind conditions were just right. For each glide, he would get a running start and then leap off into the wind. Some people thought he was crazy, but Lilienthal didn't care. Between 1891 and 1896, he made more than 2,000 flights, sometimes soaring to more than 19.5 meters (64 feet) above the ground. The longest distance he was able to glide was about 305 meters (1,000 feet). Although it may not sound like much now, it was a tremendous achievement in those days!

Inspired by the birds, Lilienthal made his gliders as lightweight as possible, using cotton fabric stretched over a light and flexible framework of willow. He gave the wings curved surfaces. Lilienthal's gliders had no steering mechanisms. The only way to steer was by shifting your weight, which was clumsy at best. Although Lilienthal was killed in a glider accident in 1896, his efforts had an enormous influence on the history of aviation. You can see an example of the most successful of Lilienthal's designs near the entrance to the gallery.

EARLY FLIGHT

Winging It

An airplane's curved wing shape is called an "airfoil." It is the wing's airfoil shape that makes lift possible.

When you're flying an airplane, the amount of lift you get depends both on the shape of the airfoil and on how the wing is angled into the air. Generally, the more angle, the more lift. But this is only up until a point; at too sharp an angle, the airplane will stall . . . and crash.

The many different wing designs of airplanes have been created to suit the different kinds of flying—higher or lower, faster or slower, upside-down or right-side-up—that planes have to do.

A great place in the museum to compare airplane wings is from the second-floor balcony, where you can get a bird's-eye view of the Milestones of Flight gallery.

After you've seen all these

The razor-sharp-edged wings of the NASA F-104 were good for slicing through the air at Mach 2 speeds (twice the speed of sound).

wings, you might like to check out the NASA Lifting Body in Space Hall. It is used for research, and the entire airplane is the wing!

Ask the Experts

About Flight

How does an airplane stay up?

Every airplane is acted on by four forces. Lift (upward force) and thrust (a forward push provided by the plane's engines) get the plane into the air. Weight (the force of gravity that keeps us all earth-bound) and drag (the friction caused by air rubbing against the plane as it moves forward) try to pull the plane down and slow its speed.

A plane must be built so that its lift and thrust are stronger than the pull of its weight and drag.

In order to get up and stay up, a plane needs air. A plane flies only if the air below its wings pushes up harder than the air above its wings pushes down. An airplane wing is curved and tilted, which forces the air traveling over the top of it to go faster than air traveling below the wing. The faster the air is traveling, the less pressure it is putting on the wing. So the slower bottom air gives the wing lift.

FOUR FORCES AFFECT THINGS THAT FLY

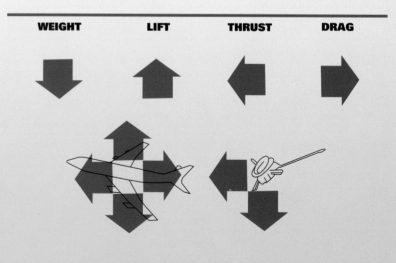

| WEIGHT | LIFT | THRUST | DRAG |

All four forces act on an airplane

Only two forces affect a spacecraft in space

HOW THE *SPIRIT OF ST. LOUIS* CAME TO WASHINGTON

Early one morning in the spring of 1927, a tall young man in a helmet and goggles stepped into the cockpit of a silver-painted airplane about twice the length of an automobile. The young man's name was Charles A. Lindbergh. His mission was to fly his airplane, the *Spirit of St. Louis,* across the Atlantic Ocean, from New York to Paris, without stopping.

Airplanes in those days were fairly new inventions and were not usually flown long distances. Most people thought that the only sensible way to cross the Atlantic—or any ocean, for that matter—was by ship. They believed Lindbergh would never make it from New York to Paris.

But thirty-three-and-a-half hours after taking off from New York, Lindbergh landed at Le Bourget Airfield outside Paris. Cheering crowds ran to meet him. The *Spirit of St. Louis* had become the first plane in the world to make a non-stop solo crossing of the Atlantic.

One of the few people who was not surprised by Lindbergh's success was Paul Garber of the Smithsonian Institution. An important part of his job was to take care of a growing collection of objects relating to flight. Because of its importance to the history of flight, Garber wanted the *Spirit of St. Louis* for the Smithsonian.

LINDBERGH IS IN PARIS

DON'T MISS IT!

From the museum balcony, you can look inside the cockpit and imagine how Lindbergh must have felt on that long-ago day when he and the *Spirit of St. Louis* set out on their grand adventure.

Top left: A Minnesota newspaper headline dated May 21, 1927, sits above a map of Lindbergh's route. Left: The $25,000 check Lindbergh received on completion of his transatlantic flight.

And so it was that when Charles Lindbergh woke up in Paris from the long sleep that followed his historic flight, a cablegram from Washington was waiting for him to read:

Smithsonian Institution congratulates you on glorious achievement. Hope *Spirit of St. Louis* will eventually join Langley's machines, the *"Army Wright"* [first plane ever owned by any government] . . . *"Chicago,"* and other historic American planes in our United States National Museum.

C.G. Abbot, Acting Secretary, Smithsonian Institution

In an interview shortly before his death in 1992, Paul Garber told us the rest of the story:

. . .On April 30, 1928, Lindbergh telephoned me and asked me to meet him at Bolling Field [outside Washington]. He was

flying the *Spirit* in and would deliver it into the Smithsonian's custody that very day! The plane was in perfect condition. We drained the gasoline from the tanks and the oil from the oil sump, and cleaned it. Then we took it apart and brought it to the Smithsonian's Arts and Industries Building, towing the body on its own wheels and carrying the wing and tail group in the truck. Here inside the museum, we put it back together and hung it from the ceiling on steel cables for visitors to see.

The *Spirit of St. Louis* was moved to the Air and Space Museum when it opened in 1976, and given a place of honor in the Milestones of Flight gallery.

Chuck Yeager and *Glamorous Glennis*

Take a small orange airplane with a bullet shape and a rocket engine, put a pilot named Chuck Yeager inside, and you have a winning combination for doing something that many people thought was impossible: flying faster than the speed of sound!

The year was 1947. The place was Muroc Field in California's Mojave Desert. Chuck Yeager was a young pilot with the Army Air Force (later to become the U.S. Air Force). His job was to test newly designed airplanes to see how they would fly. He had named his plane (an experimental Bell X-1) *Glamorous Glennis* after his wife. The Bell X-1 had been designed for a special purpose: breaking the sound barrier.

When a flying object such as an airplane approaches the speed of sound within the earth's atmosphere, powerful shock waves are produced. These shock waves had been known to shake a plane so hard that it fell apart or went completely out of the pilot's control . . . and crashed.

The Bell X-1 was like no other plane Yeager had ever flown. Instead of taking off from the ground on its own power, it was carried aloft underneath the belly of a B-29 bomber and then launched. During the early practice flights, Yeager glided back to Earth without firing the plane's rocket engines. Later he began using the engines to push the plane higher and higher, faster and faster. He was getting closer and closer to the speed of sound, roughly 1120 kilometers (700 miles) per hour, or Mach 1.

Finally, on October 14, 1947, the day arrived. *Glamorous Glennis* and Chuck Yeager would try to break the sound barrier. What few people knew was that Yeager had broken something else the night before! Riding in the desert, he had fractured two ribs when he fell off his horse. He was in a lot of pain, but he decided to go ahead with the flight anyway.

In his autobiography, Chuck Yeager later described what it felt like to fly at supersonic speed for the very first time:

Suddenly the Mach needle began to fluctuate. It went up to .965 Mach—then tipped right off the scale. I thought I was seeing things! And it was as smooth as a baby's bottom: Grandma could be up there sipping lemonade. I kept the speed off the scale for about twenty seconds. Then I raised the nose to slow down.

Amazing But True
What's Up, Mach?

A Mach number measures the speed of a moving body—such as an airplane—in relation to the speed of sound. When an airplane reaches Mach 1, it is flying at the speed of sound, about 1120 kilometers (700 miles) per hour. Mach 2 is twice the speed of sound—about 2240 kilometers (or 1400 miles) per hour—and so on. When a Mach number is greater than 1, it means the moving body is going at supersonic (faster than sound) speed. The term is named for the Austrian physicist Ernst Mach (1838-1916), who studied the movement of objects at high speeds.

A few minutes later, *Glamorous Glennis* glided in for a perfect landing. In 1950, the U.S. Air Force gave *Glamorous Glennis* to the Smithsonian. And in 1976, when the Air and Space Museum opened, the airplane joined the legendary stars in the Milestones of Flight gallery. Among the those who come to admire her, we sometimes see General Chuck Yeager stopping by to say hello.

Visitors to Mars—The Vikings Land

At one corner of Milestones of Flight is a long-legged contraption that looks something like a giant insect. It is the test model for a kind of robot known as the Viking Lander. Two identical Viking Landers went to the planet Mars in the 1970s.

For hundreds of years, people had been curious about Mars. Along with Venus, Mars is one of Earth's closest neighboring planets.

Back around 1900, when telescopes still provided our only means of getting a closer look at the planets, some astronomers thought that Mars was inhabited. Peering through their telescopes, they saw lines criss-crossing the planet's surface that looked to them like canals filled with water. They reasoned that if Mars had water and irrigation systems, then intelligent beings probably existed there.

And scientists weren't the only ones with ideas about Mars. Science fiction writers wove fabulous tales of bug-eyed monsters or little green men that excited people's curiosity.

In the 1970s, many people hoped that there might be some form of life on Mars. Scientists figured that if living things did exist on Mars, they would most likely be so small that you would need a microscope to see them. But the prospect of finding any kind of life on Mars— even the teeniest, tiniest form— was exciting.

When Vikings 1 and 2 went rocketing off into space about a month apart, in August and September, 1975, everyone wanted to know: What would these two missions to Mars tell us?

The vehicles (each consisting of an orbiter/lander combination) entered Martian orbit about eight months after launch. In orbit, one of their jobs was to photograph the planet's surface. The resulting pictures, radioed back to Earth, showed craters, valleys, huge volcanic mountains, and ancient, dried-up river beds. Everything had a reddish tinge. It was a landscape that looked a lot like the desert in our own American Southwest. In July and September, 1976, the two Viking Landers detached from their orbiters and touched down at two different locations. It was the first time in human history that spacecraft had ever landed and operated successfully on Mars!

The two robotic landers took close-up photographs of the planet's surface, measured the speed and direction of the wind, and gathered soil samples. The results, along with all the other scientific data collected, were radioed back to Earth. But the tests revealed no living things— not even the smallest microorganisms.

The Viking 1 and 2 Landers are still on Mars, exactly where they touched down in 1976. One of the landers stopped transmitting four years later. But, for six-and-a-half years after landing, the other lander continued to radio photographs and other information back to Earth every once in a while. Then it fell silent. We haven't heard from it since 1982, and the question remains: Is there now, or has there ever been, life on Mars? We still don't know for sure.

One trouble with the Viking Landers was that they had to stay right where they landed because they didn't have any means of moving around. So the soil samples they gathered came from just two very limited areas. Evidence of life—past or present—may still exist elsewhere on Mars.

DON'T MISS IT!

TOUCH THE MOON

There are only two places in the entire world where you can walk in the door and touch a piece of the Moon. One of them is the Johnson Space Center in Houston, Texas, and the other is the National Air and Space Museum.

The Moonrock is just a small chunk of the 109 kilograms (243 pounds) of rock picked up by the Apollo 17 astronauts in 1972. Scientists estimate that it is nearly 4 billion years old, which means that it well may be the oldest thing you touch in your whole lifetime!

Moonrock samples like this one—and others you can find upstairs in the Apollo to the Moon exhibition—have provided scientists with clues about what the Moon is made of and how old it is.

THE SPACE MURAL

If you enter the Air and Space Museum from Independence Avenue, you can't miss it: the space mural is 22.5 meters (75 feet) wide, and the vertical section is 18 meters (58.5 feet) high! Robert McCall painted this mural for the new museum in 1976 to celebrate the wonders of the universe and our human quest to explore it. The mural begins on the left with an explosion of energy signaling the creation of the universe. As your eyes follow a pathway of stars, you arrive at the planets of our own solar system. In the center of the mural, an astronaut plants a large American flag on the Moon. The visor of the astronaut's space helmet reflects stars and the blackness of space, making him part of the cosmos he surveys. The vertical section of the mural (not shown here) depicts the rising sun and galaxies of stars, including our own Milky Way. According to the artist Robert McCall, ". . . no single event has shaped man's future so profoundly as the landing of the American astronauts on the Moon. In that brief moment, man's vision shifted for all time from earthly horizons to include the planets and the stars."

HIGHWAYS IN THE SKIES

When airplanes were
first invented, many people found them
exciting, but hardly anybody understood their practical
value. Few people could foresee a time when airplanes would be carrying people and
cargo long distances. In fact, it wasn't until well into the 1920s (more than twenty
years after the Wright brothers flew) that the airplane became widely accepted as a vehicle
that could do important work.

In the first-floor gallery called Air Transportation you can see some of the airplanes that,
from the 1920s through the 1950s, led the way for future air passengers like you and me.

FLYING THE MAIL

In the 1920s, when airmail service was still very new, only the best pilots could qualify to fly the mail, and the public looked up to them as heroes.

With no radar and no computers to help with navigation, flying through fog and storms was extremely dangerous.

Engines weren't reliable, either, and a pilot never knew when his engine might conk out, forcing a crash landing. Yet, no matter how great the danger, the mail had to get through.

In the Air Transportation gallery you can see two airmail planes. The 1927 black and yellow Pitcairn Mailwing (shown above) delivered mail between

New York and Atlanta in the late 1920s and 1930s. A 1926 silver and red Douglas M-2 Mailplane is exhibited as part of a large diorama showing a pilot unloading the mail at one of his stops.

POWERFUL PISTONS, MIGHTY JETS

An airplane's engine provides the thrust that pushes the airplane forward. In the Air Transportation gallery, there is an entire exhibit of airplane engines lined up in a row. The piston engine was developed first. In fact, all airplanes used piston engines until the 1940s. Many smaller airplanes still use them today.

A piston engine generally has three or more "cylinders." Inside each cylinder is a piston connected to the airplane's crankshaft, as well as a combustion chamber. When air and fuel mix and are ignited by a spark inside the combustion chamber, energy is released, which drives the piston up and down. This happens simultaneously in all of the airplane's cylinders. The movement of the piston turns the crankshaft, which, in turn, turns the propeller, which pulls the airplane forward.

The jet engine first came into use during World War II, although it was not used commercially until the late 1950s. Jet engines work better than piston engines at high speeds and altitudes.

The GE Turbofan jet engine is used on many of today's passenger jets. In the exhibition you can set in motion an important jet engine device called a "compressor." When you push the button, the compressor will start spinning around. Although you can't see it, the job of the compressor is to draw air into the engine, compress it, and mix it with fuel. The mixture of air and fuel is then ignited, creating hot gas. The gas is forced out through an opening in the engine's tail end, pushing the airplane forward. This is, essentially, how all jet engines work. (To find out more, take a look at exhibits in the entrance to the Jet Aviation gallery, directly across from Air Transportation.)

AMAZING BUT TRUE

WHOOSH . . . A GOOSE!

In 1936, some wealthy businessmen asked the Grumman Aircraft Engineering Corporation to design an airplane that would whisk them from their homes on Long Island to their offices in New York City. Grumman came up with the G-21, otherwise known as the "Grumman Goose." Besides comfort and reliability, an important feature of the G-21 was that it could take off and land from the water, like—you guessed it—a goose. As an added bonus, its main and tail wheels could be replaced with skis for landing on snow.

During World War II, the Goose was put to work by the U.S. military for everything from flying targets to patrolling for submarines to taking aerial photographs. Today a retired Grumman Goose occupies a place of honor in the Air Transportation gallery.

Interior view of a
Pratt and Whitney
R-985 "Wasp Junior"
piston engine.

First the Dream...
Then the Reality

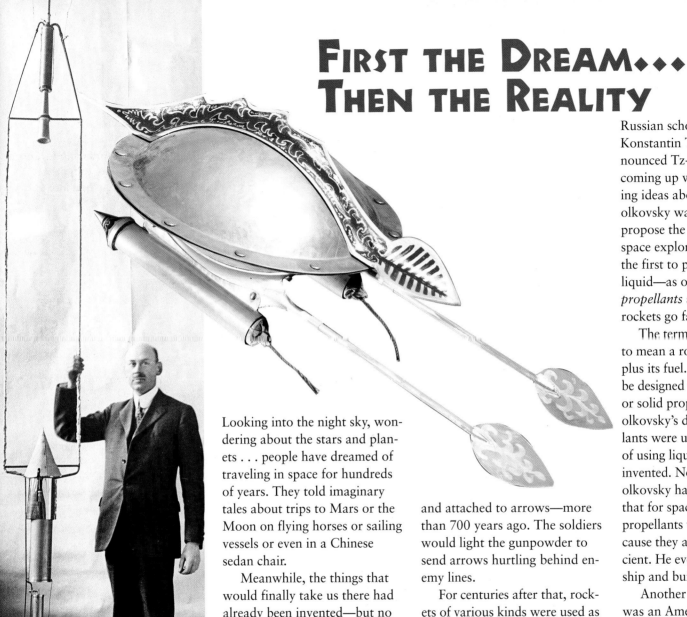

Looking into the night sky, wondering about the stars and planets . . . people have dreamed of traveling in space for hundreds of years. They told imaginary tales about trips to Mars or the Moon on flying horses or sailing vessels or even in a Chinese sedan chair.

Meanwhile, the things that would finally take us there had already been invented—but no one realized it. Rockets have been around a long time, though often very diffferent from those we have today. Chinese soldiers used rockets similar to the Arabian one shown above—bamboo tubes, capped at one end

and attached to arrows—more than 700 years ago. The soldiers would light the gunpowder to send arrows hurtling behind enemy lines.

For centuries after that, rockets of various kinds were used as weapons of war, and also as fireworks. But it wasn't until the late 1800s that the age of modern rocketry began.

Around the same time that the Wright brothers were experimenting with airplanes, a

Russian schoolteacher named Konstantin Tsiolkovsky (pronounced Tz-ee-ol-kov-skee) was coming up with some very exciting ideas about rockets. Tsiolkovsky was the first person to propose the use of rockets for space exploration. He was also the first to propose the use of liquid—as opposed to solid—*propellants* as a way of making rockets go faster and farther.

The term "propellant" is used to mean a rocket's oxygen supply plus its fuel. Today's rockets can be designed to use either liquid or solid propellants. In Tsiolkovsky's day, only solid propellants were used, because a way of using liquids had not yet been invented. Nonetheless, Tsiolkovsky had the vision to see that for space exploration, liquid propellants would be better because they are more energy efficient. He even designed a rocket ship and built a model.

Another pioneer of rocketry was an American named Robert H. Goddard (in photo at left). Goddard shared Tsiolkovsky's vision that rockets would one day take people into outer space. He too became convinced that a rocket could be propelled more efficiently by liquid fuel.

A view of Space Hall, showing rockets in the missile pit.

Ask the Experts... About Rockets

How does a rocket work?

If you've ever taken a balloon, blown it up, and then let go, you know what happens next. The balloon takes off! And believe it or not, this is just about the same thing that happens when a rocket is launched into space. Both the balloon and the rocket are filled with gas. The gas is under pressure. When the gas escapes through the nozzle in one end, the balloon or the rocket is pushed (or propelled) forward. Zoom!

There is, however, one big difference between the rocket and the balloon. The difference lies in the way the gas inside the rocket is produced. In the case of the balloon, you put the gas there with your own breath. In the case of the rocket, the gas is produced by burning fuel.

Why does the space program use rockets?

Without rockets and rocket engines, space exploration would not be possible. Jet airplanes cannot venture into space because their engines need oxygen from the atmosphere in order to work. In space there is no atmosphere and therefore no oxygen. To a rocket engine, however, the lack of oxygen does not matter— because rockets carry their own oxygen with them, in the form of an oxidizer. When the oxidizer is mixed with the rocket's fuel, combustion takes place, creating gasses that build up under pressure and then escape . . . and the rocket takes off.

While Tsiolkovsky was the first to propose this idea, Goddard was the first to try it out successfully.

Designing and building the first liquid-propellant rocket presented some very big challenges: how could one keep the engine cool? How could the propellants be moved from their storage tanks to the combustion chamber? Finally, on March 16, 1926, after six years of experimentation and hard work,

Goddard launched a liquid-propellant rocket 12.5 meters (43 feet) into the air! The flight lasted only 2.5 seconds, but it marked an important beginning. Even though none of Goddard's rockets ever made it into space, they paved the way for rockets that *did* make it, starting in the 1950s.

From dream to reality, all in the twentieth century. Thanks to the vision and hard work of these early pioneers the age of modern rocketry—and later of space flight travel—finally got off the ground!

A GIANT LEAP

Astronaut Buzz
Aldrin's visor reflects
Apollo 11's lunar
module and the pho-
tographer, fellow as-
tronaut Neil Arm-
strong.

One of the most popular objects in Space Hall is a strange-looking exploring machine called a "lunar lander." It is exactly like the machine in which two men—Neil A. Armstrong and Edwin "Buzz" Aldrin—became the first people ever to land on the Moon, on July 20, 1969.

Four days earlier, Armstrong, Aldrin, and a third astronaut named Michael Collins had climbed into a spacecraft in Cape Kennedy, Florida, fastened their seat belts, and prepared for lift-off. Their mission was called Apollo 11. The spacecraft they would fly in consisted of three parts:

◆ a small command module called *Columbia*, in which the astronauts would work, eat, and sleep on their way to and from the Moon;

◆ a service module, in which fuel, as well as power-generating equipment and other instruments were stored;

◆ a lunar module called *Eagle,* in which two of the astronauts would land on the Moon.

To get to the Moon, the spacecraft—with the astronauts inside—hitched a ride on top of an enormous Saturn V rocket. 10, 9, 8, 7, 6, 5, 4, 3, 2, 1. Lift-off! Saturn V thundered up off its launch pad, trailing smoke and fire. The ground trembled for miles around. Shaking, rattling, and swaying, Apollo 11 was off to the Moon.

On the way to the Moon, the three astronauts had to perform the dangerous and difficult task of separating the *Eagle* from the *Columbia,* turning *Columbia* around, and joining the two vehicles nose to nose. Armstrong and Aldrin then had to climb through the nose of the *Columbia* into the *Eagle* and land it on the Moon. While Armstrong and Aldrin got out and explored, Collins orbited the Moon in the *Columbia*. Less than twenty-four hours later, Armstrong and Aldrin were safely back inside the command module, and the three men were headed back to Earth.

It would be three more days before their splashdown in the Atlantic Ocean—and a very long time before the excitemnet over their historic feat died down. Today we still look back and marvel at the skill and bravery of the Apollo 11 astronauts and at the technology that took them to the Moon and brought them back to Earth.

DON'T MISS IT!

Don't miss seeing the actual Apollo 11 command module in the Milestones of Flight gallery. And up on the second floor, adventure and exploration are yours for the asking in a gallery called Apollo to the Moon (see pp. 140-141). Here you can see the Apollo astronauts at work on the Moon and in their space capsules. You can learn about the food they ate, the clothes they wore, the tools they used, the vehicles they flew in, the discoveries they made . . . and more. You can even join them in the Apollo 17 spacecraft to help pilot the last landing ever made on the Moon.

MICHAEL COLLINS' SECRET MESSAGE

SPACECRAFT 107, ALIAS APOLLO 11, ALIAS COLUMBIA. THE BEST SHIP TO COME DOWN THE LINE. GOD BLESS HER,

[SIGNED] MICHAEL COLLINS, C.M.P.

*C.M.P. stands for "Command Module Pilot

Some time after the Apollo 11 flight, astronaut Michael Collins returned to the *Columbia*. Climbing inside, he wrote the message above to record the affection and regard he and his fellow astronauts felt for that small but sturdy vehicle.

Because Michael Collins' message is not visible from outside the spacecraft, where it is exhibited in Milestones of Flight, few museum visitors know it's there. It's a secret you can share with your friends.

BRINGING IT ALL BACK HOME

On the morning of April 10, 1981, the beaches and causeways around the Kennedy Space Center were crowded with over 600,000 spectators. They had come to see the launch of *Columbia*, the first space shuttle.

In Space Hall, you can see a 1:15 scale model of the space shuttle on its launch pad. The gleaming white shuttle orbiter is attached to a huge tan fuel tank, filled with liquid hydrogen and liquid oxygen. This tank feeds three powerful rocket engines at the base of the orbiter. On either side of the fuel tank are rocket boosters filled with solid fuel, which have engines of their own. The engines and the boosters fire within seconds of each other to launch the shuttle into space.

Just like earlier astronauts, shuttle crews have to endure a bone-rattling, teeth-jarring ride on a column of fire. But unlike previous space vehicles, almost all of the shuttle can be reused. All the fuel in the solid rocket boosters is used up in the first two minutes of flight. Then they fall away from the shuttle into the ocean, where they are retrieved and prepared for reuse on another flight. Most wonderful of all, at the end of the mission, the orbiter glides back to Earth under the control of its pilot, and lands smoothly on a runway. There are four orbiters in the present fleet—*Columbia, Discovery, Atlantis,* and *Endeavor.* (*Challenger* was destroyed in a tragic launch accident in 1986.)

Each shuttle mission lasts about a week. The crew—usually five to seven people—keeps busy with a tight schedule of activities. Some missions launch satellites into orbit; others pick them up for repair and return to Earth. On some missions, a science lab is fitted into the cargo bay of the orbiter, and scientists work in shifts around the clock to carry out as many experiments as they can. Several missions have taken IMAX cameras with them, to share with us the ever-changing panorama of planet Earth visible from the shuttle. Perhaps one day you'll be part of a shuttle crew and see the breath-taking view for yourself.

The shuttle has opened up space to many more people than ever before. The earliest astronauts were all white men who had been test pilots. Today women and Americans of every race can share in the dream. Some missions have an international flavor: Canadians, Germans, Japanese, and crew members of many other nationalities have worked closely with Americans aboard the shuttle. Since that first launch in 1981, the shuttle fleet has made over 70 more voyages, carrying almost 200 men and women on the greatest adventure of their lives.

In this scene from the IMAX film *Destiny in Space,* shown on the big screen in the Samuel P. Langley Theater, shuttle astronauts work in orbit 200 miles above Earth.

Science in Space

Skylab was America's first space station. For a total of five-and-a-half months in 1973 and 1974, three three-man teams of astronauts worked in Skylab conducting scientific experiments. Each team arrived in an Apollo spacecraft and docked at Skylab's forward end. Upon finishing their assignments after several weeks, the astronauts got back into their spacecraft and returned to Earth . . . and the next team moved in and took over.

For many space missions, identical backup models of spacecraft were made to be used in case something happened to the original. If you climb the stairs to the museum's second floor, right above Space Hall, you can see—and go inside—the backup model to Skylab's Orbital Workshop, where the astronauts lived and worked.

Right away you'll notice that even though the workshop does not look very cozy, it had many of the comforts of home. If you compare this living space to the one the Apollo astronauts had just a few years earlier, you can see that Skylab had a lot more room. It had separate areas for eating and sleeping—and even a toilet and a shower! These features enabled the astronauts to remain in space longer and to get more work done, gathering information for scientists back on Earth to study.

One of the most important areas of Skylab research was to observe and photograph the Sun. Using eight telescopes and several special cameras, the astronauts took hundreds of pictures of the Sun, showing it to be a much more active star than scientists had ever realized.

Scientists were also eager to find out the effects on the human body of living in space. They knew that the future of manned spaceflight would depend on whether people could adjust to weightlessness, remain healthy in space, and not suffer any lasting health problems after returning to Earth. Even though motion sickness was a problem for some of the astronauts, overall the men remained healthy, showing that long space missions were indeed possible.

The astronauts also performed many other experiments. One of these was designed by an American high-school student. It looked at the effects of weightlessness on the ability of a spider to spin a web. The spider's name was Arabella. After several days of not knowing up from down, Arabella managed to regain her bearings—and spun her webs perfectly!

Finally, on February 8, 1974, the Skylab missions were over. The last crew packed up its scientific data and returned to Earth. But that is not the end of the story. Skylab itself remained in orbit for five more years, slowly losing altitude. When it finally began its descent to Earth, many people became nervous. Nobody knew where it would fall, and there was concern that somebody might get hurt. A company called Chicken Little Associates was even formed. For a fee, they would tell you the likelihood of Skylab falling on *you!*

Then on July 11, 1979, Skylab plunged in pieces into the Indian Ocean and a remote part of Australia. Fortunately no one was hurt. However, the people who lived in that part of Australia reported a display of bright lights, sonic booms, and loud whirring noises as the chunks passed overhead in the early morning darkness, marking the end of America's first great scientific laboratory in the sky.

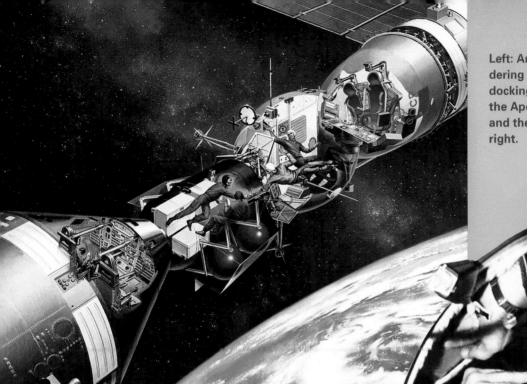

Left: An artist's rendering of the historic docking in space, with the Apollo on the left and the Soyuz on the right.

Below: Astronaut Thomas P. Stafford and Cosmonaut Aleksey A. Leonov in the hatchway connecting the Apollo's docking module and the Soyuz spacecraft's Orbital Module.

AMAZING BUT TRUE
ASTRONAUT MEETS COSMONAUT ♦ ♦ ♦ IN SPACE

On July 17, 1975, about a year and a half after the last team of Skylab astronauts returned to Earth, the United States and the Soviet Union made an historic link-up in space.

At the time, they were the only two countries in the world to have manned space programs, and each wanted to be the best. Their heated competition was known as "the space race."

But on that day in 1975, the two countries put the space race aside in a spirit of international cooperation. An Apollo space-craft carrying three American astronauts docked with a Soyuz spacecraft carrying two Soviet cosmonauts. For the next two days, the men shared meals, exchanged gifts, and conducted joint scientific experiments.

This exercise paved the way for international cooperation in space, which continues until this day as many nations join forces on space missions.

FROM SLIDE RULES TO COMPUTERS

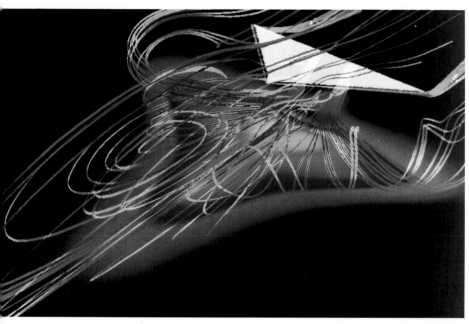

DON'T MISS IT!

In Beyond the Limits, you can pretend to be a modern aircraft designer yourself, at a real computer work station. Other interactives let you test, build, navigate, and even fly modern aircraft. All you need is a computer—and your imagination.

This supercomputer-generated image shows the flow of air over an airfoil as it lifts off.

What do a Mickey Mouse calculator, a pocket Nintendo game, and a supersonic X-29 airplane have in common? You can find the answers to this and other questions in a new second-floor exhibition called Beyond the Limits: Flight Enters the Computer Age.

When the Wright brothers designed the first airplane in 1903, there were no computers. A few individuals had to do all the mathematical calculations by hand and create precisely detailed sketches and line drawings. Such painstaking methods were used in aircraft design for the next forty years.

Then came World War II (1939-1945). Airplanes were so important to the war effort that a lot of money was spent to improve them. But the new faster, sturdier, and more agile airplanes were also much more complicated to design.

New design methods had to be adopted by the growing postwar aerospace industry. At first, the work was simply divided among teams of men and women. The men made the blueprints and sketches, while the women processed the numbers on desktop calculators.

In the 1950s computers were introduced, but the technology was still new and limited to numerical processing. In the 1970s, more sophisticated machines were developed that could handle drawings as well.

A 1970s "supercomputer" called the CRAY 1 can be seen in Beyond the Limits. The CRAY 1 could accomplish in seconds work it would have taken the Wright brothers weeks, or even months, to do. Once computers could handle both numbers processing and graphics production, designers gave up the old-fashioned tools of their trade—slide rules and drafting tables—in favor of computer work stations.

Today, designers can even build tiny computer chips right into the control panel or the engine of an aircraft. These "intelligent" vehicles may not need a human pilot at all, but can actually fly themselves, or be controlled from the ground.

Hot Air Ride

Did you know that the first machine to fly with humans aboard was not an airplane or a glider—but a hot air balloon?

The date of this historic flight was November 21, 1783. The place was Paris, France. For twenty-five minutes the giant blue, red, and yellow craft floated over the city while crowds of people watched in amazement. Riding in a basket suspended beneath the balloon were two French noblemen, Pilatre de Rozier and the Marquis d'Arlandes. They were dressed for the occasion in powdered wigs and fancy topcoats.

To get the balloon off the ground, the two men lit a fire in a grate attached to the entrance of the balloon's open neck. Hot air filled the balloon—and because the hot air was less dense than the cooler air outside the balloon's envelope, the balloon rose up . . . and up . . . and up.

Once aloft, the trick was to keep the air inside the envelope hot so that the balloon would *stay* up. This meant continually stoking the fire, even though at any moment the fire in the grate might spread to the envelope, ending the flight in disaster!

It was to minimize this risk that the men limited the flight to twenty-five minutes. When the time was up, they stopped stoking the fire—and down they went to a safe landing.

In Pioneers of Flight you can see a 1/4-scale model of this famous craft, called the "Montgolfier Balloon" after its inventors, Joseph and Etienne Montgolfier.

Amazing But True
Better Than A Bird

The world's slowest airplane is also the lightest in weight . . . and you can find it in Pioneers of Flight. Built of plastic sheeting, adhesive tape, cardboard, toy wagon wheels, bicycle pedals, and other everyday materials, it is called the Gossamer Condor. A condor is a kind of bird. "Gossamer" means sheer and light.

Despite its flimsy, makeshift appearance and a top speed of only 17.5 kilometers (11 miles) per hour, the Gossamer Condor has an important claim to fame. In 1977, in this small airplane, pilot Bryan Allen (shown at left on a test flight) made the first successful attempt to realize the age-old dream of human-powered flight.

Huffing and puffing, Allen pumped the Condor's pedals harder and harder until, solely under his own muscle power, he managed to get the airplane off the ground and to fly it for 6 minutes and 22 seconds on a 0.8-kilometer (0.5-mile) course.

From Seattle to Seattle ••• in 130 Days

On April 6, 1924, eight adventuresome young men set out in four small airplanes to make the very first around-the-world flight.

In the Pioneers of Flight gallery, you can see pictures of these men, a map of the route they took, and one of the planes they flew. The plane is called the Douglas World Cruiser *Chicago*. In 130 days, it and another plane, the *New Orleans,* flew 44,000 kilometers (27,553 miles), beginning and ending in Seattle and making sixty-five stops along the way. Although four planes set out in the beginning, only the *Chicago* and the *New Orleans* made it through to the end.

Each plane held two people: a pilot and a mechanic. For some of the trip, the planes were outfitted with pontoons for water take-offs and landings.

In those days flying around the world was a much bigger challenge than it is today. For one thing, the open cockpits that airplanes had then gave the crew almost no protection from the weather. For another, airplanes couldn't go as fast as they can now. Their average speed was 145 kilometers (90 miles) per hour as compared to 560 kilometers (350 miles) per hour for today's passenger jet. Also, frequent, time-consuming stops were necessary—for resting and refueling, making airplane repairs, and waiting out storms.

To make matters worse, it was often impossible to know where you were going—or even whether you were flying right-side up! With just a compass and a map to guide you, you could easily get lost or crash into something, especially in bad weather. Without the help of radar, which hadn't been invented in 1924, it was easy to lose your orientation when you couldn't see the ground. Many a pilot would come flying out of a cloud bank upside-down, without knowing it!

Is it any wonder, then, that only two of the four World Cruisers made it all the way back to Seattle?

The two planes that *didn't* make it were the *Seattle* and the *Boston*. The *Seattle* went down first. Lost in fog, it crashed into an Alaskan mountainside just three weeks into the trip. Three months later the *Boston* went down when a broken oil pump forced it to land in the North Atlantic. In both cases, the crews were unharmed, but the airplanes were damaged beyond repair.

Meanwhile the *New Orleans* and the *Chicago* pressed on. On November 24, 1924, they finally made it to Seattle. Cheering crowds greeted them, and newspaper reporters from around the world rushed in to cover the event. President Grover Cleveland sent a telegram saying thanks on behalf of the entire United States. Because of the bravery and stamina of eight young men, the world had suddenly become a much smaller place.

Four pictures of the *Chicago,* standing in for the four planes that began the race. Of the four, only the *Chicago* and the *New Orleans* finished the journey.

Right: A period poster shows six of the men who made the round-the-world flight (and a not-very-accurate map of their route).

Amelia Earhart's Soaring Adventures

Amelia Earhart was halfway across the Atlantic on the night of May 20, 1932. She was determined to become the first woman to make a solo flight across the ocean, but she already knew it wasn't going to be easy. Amelia's altimeter—the instrument that told her how high she was flying—had failed. Then her small Lockheed Vega hit the roughest weather she had ever encountered. She was flying blind through inky storm clouds, her small plane bucking so hard that she couldn't be sure she was still on course. When she tried to climb above the storm, her plane began to pick up a deadly coat of ice.

Before the ice could drag her plane out of the sky, Amelia flew low to melt it off—so low that she could see the whitecaps on the stormy ocean before she leveled out. With no altimeter to warn her she was too low, she had almost plunged into the sea.

Through it all, Amelia kept cool, concentrating on her goal and waiting for dawn. With only a little fuel left, she finally sighted the coast of Ireland. On the morning of May 21, 14 hours and 54 minutes after she had left Harbour Grace, Newfoundland, Amelia set down her plane in a farmer's field outside Londonderry. She taxied right up to the startled man's door and asked if she could have a drink of water!

Amelia was already a celebrated pilot when she made this historic flight, but now she was world famous, and everything she did was news. Later in 1932, she flew across the United States, and in 1934, she flew across the Pacific Ocean. Soon she was making plans for her greatest adventure of all. On March 17, 1937, with co-pilot Fred Noonan, Amelia set out to fly around the world. But her skill or her luck—probably no one will ever know which—finally failed her. In

HOPE FADES FOR AMELIA STORMS BLOCK SEARCH

Los Angeles Men Insist They Heard Miss Earhart's Voice Calling Out an SOS

July, her twin-engine Electra went down in the South Pacific. Although a huge search was made, no trace of Amelia or Fred or the plane was found. What happened remains one of the world's greatest mysteries.

Maybe one day Amelia's Electra will be recovered, since there are still people who have not given up looking for it. In the meantime, you can see her bright red Vega (shown above), in which she made her record-breaking flights across the Atlantic and across the United States. Amelia Earhart proved to the entire world that aviation was not just for men. She showed that women were strong and resourceful and could soar as high as their dreams and their daring would take them.

QUEEN BESS

Queen Bess, the "daring aviatrix," was one of the bravest airshow pilots of the 1920s. At this time, planes were still a novelty for most Americans, and "flying circus" pilots thrilled crowds at county fairs with death-defying stunts. Queen Bess performed dazzling loop-the-loops, figure eights, and barrel rolls in the flimsy old plane that was all she could afford.

Nothing in her life had ever come easily to Bessie Coleman. At a time when any woman who wanted to fly faced discrimination, Bessie had a much harder time because she was a woman of color. Bessie was licensed as a pilot in 1921, two years before Amelia Earhart. But she had to go all the way to France to get her training. No American flight school at that time would accept her. She became the first African American to earn an international pilot's license and the first black woman in the world to fly an airplane. Bessie's life was tragically brief—ended by a flying accident in 1926 when she was only 34. But as African American astronaut Mae Jemison—herself a trailblazer—put it, "I am convinced that the fall from the airplane that killed her did not kill her spirit . . . Because what Bessie Coleman affirms is the *life* in each of us."

Bessie Coleman in front of the Nieuport plane in which she learned to fly.

You on the Moon

As you walk through the Apollo to the Moon exhibit on the second floor, you can use your imagination to get an idea of what being on the Moon would be like, not only for the Apollo astronauts, but for you too.

Just imagine a place with no air and virtually no water. With no air, there's no wind, and with no water, there's no erosion. On Earth, wind and water are constantly reshaping the landscape. But on the Moon, a footprint you leave today will still be there a day from now . . . a year from now . . . even a *million* years from now!

No air and no water also means no life. The Moon has no birds, no flowers, no trees, no insects, and, of course, no people. For "tourist attractions," the Moon has nothing except hills, ridges, rills, and craters, covered with rocks and loose, dry soil. Further, the Moon is a completely silent place—for without air, there is no way for sound waves to travel.

Having no air on the Moon means other things as well. For one thing, without atmosphere to filter it, the light of the Sun is enor-

mously bright. Shadows are very dark, with sharp edges. During the day it is extremely hot (121°C/250°F). At night it is extremely cold (-121°C/-250°F), and the stars shine brilliantly.

It's a good thing your space suit not only has its own oxygen supply but also its own heating and cooling system, plus a visor to shield your eyes from the Sun's blinding rays. Without this special suit of clothing, you would not be able to survive on the Moon for even a few seconds.

Stepping out on the Moon, you feel like a lightweight, and in fact you are. Owing to the Moon's much weaker gravitational pull, the weight of everything on the Moon—including you—is only one-sixth as much as on Earth. You'll have as much spring in your step as if you were on a trampoline!

After you've been on the Moon for about seven hours, collecting rocks and surveying the landscape, your spacesuit's battery-powered life-support system will begin to run down. It's time to climb back into your spacecraft and return home to Earth.

Above: The plastic food packages on the left are the kind carried on Apollo missions. They are equal to the "Earth meal" shown on the right. the water gun on the lower left was used to make the dehydrated (dried out) space food edible.

Left: This woman is modeling a liquid-cooled undergarment similar to the one worn by the Apollo astronauts.

Ask the Experts
ABOUT THE APOLLO MISSIONS

Why were the Apollo missions called "Apollo?"
The missions were named after the Greek god, Apollo. In Greek mythology, Apollo was the Sun god. He was also the archer god, who could send arrows flying long distances with great accuracy. Among the ideals he stood for were beauty, light, and truth.

What did the Apollo astronauts eat?
Chicken soup, shrimp, peanut cubes, chocolate pudding, and coffee were a few of the menu items. Since the astronauts were in a weightless environment, all of the food had to be dried and stored in plastic packets so it wouldn't float around the cabin. The astronauts fixed their meals by squirting water into a hole in one end of the plastic packet. Then they ate the food directly out of the packet.

How did they sleep?
Zipped up in floating hammocks that were tethered to the inside of the cabin.

What did they wear?
While taking off and landing, they wore a helmet and a protective suit. Made of twenty-one layers of insulating material, the suit was hooked up to the command module's oxygen supply and other life-support systems. During the flight, they wore simple coveralls, with no life-support system attached. On the Moon, they donned an outfit similar to the one worn for take-off and landing. The main difference was that the suit had an additional outer layer of material to protect them against micro-meteorites. (These are grains of dust and other small particles moving through space at such high speeds that they could drill right through an unshielded astronaut.) This suit was also hooked up to a portable life-support system. The helmet was made of extra strong plastic; while walking on the Moon, the astronauts also wore an outer visor to shield against eye-damaging radiation.

INTO THE UNKNOWN

Where Next, Columbus?, a new exhibition on the museum's second floor, looks at the past 500 years of human exploration, from before Christopher Columbus's time up to the present day and on into the future. And all along the way, you get to be an explorer yourself.

The exhibition is divided into four main parts:

◆ **Exploring This World** takes you back in time to look at the *history* of exploration, starting with Columbus's voyages and leading up through the Apollo Moon missions of the 1960s and 1970s.

◆ **Challenges for Space Explorers** shows you that in the second half of the twentieth century we have become a spacefaring people. But space travel to other worlds is harder than orbiting Earth or going to the Moon. Longer voyages—to Mars, for example—present even tougher challenges. In this part of the exhibition, you get to decide—with the help of computer interactives—whether further space exploration is worth the effort.

◆ **Exploring New Worlds** lets you compare the two basic means we have of exploring the planets—by sending human beings or by sending robots. The site is a realistic Martian landscape. You'll get to try your hand at designing a robot to send to Mars . . . and at planning your own personal Mars mission.

◆ **To the Stars**, the exhibition's final section, gives you a chance to stargaze in Earth's own galaxy, the Milky Way. Inside a special "stellarium," you'll see that even the stars closest to Earth are a lot farther away than the planets in our own solar system. In this part of the exhibition, you'll also get to consider the question of extraterrestrial intelligence. An electronic game helps you to think about whether other civilizations exist in our galaxy. In addition, you can use a computer screen to find out what some experts think. You may be surprised by their answers!

Before leaving the exhibition, stop at the public opinion poll station where you can register your own ideas about exploring the universe, and compare your opinions with those of other visitors.

Don't Miss It!

Where Next, Columbus? features three ten-minute films produced especially with kids in mind. "Other Worlds" gives you a breathtaking view of our solar system. "Spacefaring" lets you watch space adventure movies with Albert Einstein. And "Contact" asks you to consider: what are your own hopes and fears about making contact with extraterrestrials?

Boldly Going: The Space Robots

Robots are machines that take the place of people. They do things we cannot—or don't want to—do. Robots are used a lot in planetary exploration.

So far, the Moon is the only place in space where human beings have actually set foot. Robots—mostly from the former Soviet Union and the U.S.—have done all the rest of the exploring. Few of these robots have landed on a planet, however. Most have conducted their explorations from afar. Through "fly-by" and "orbiter" missions, they have photographed the planets' surfaces and probed their atmospheres.

The realistic Martian landscape—complete with human and robotic explorers—of the Where Next, Columbus? exhibit.

Behind the Scenes
Making Mars Real

How did the museum make the Mars section of Where Next, Columbus? look so real? To find out, we interviewed Valerie Neal, the scholar who curated the exhibition, and William Jacobs, the principal designer. Together they led the team of people who created Where Next, Columbus?

A lot of research went into figuring out what Mars should look like, they told us. First they chose a site on Mars that seemed especially well suited to be a base from which both robots and astronauts could explore. This location—known as *Kasei Valles*—is in a protected valley, contains lots of interesting geological features, and is a likely place to find fossils if, indeed, there *are* any fossils on Mars.

Next Neal and Jacobs studied information that had been collected from 1976 to l982 during the Viking Mars mission (see pp. 120-121): photographs of mountains, valleys, and craters as well as data about wind velocity, soil composition, and surface temperatures. Discussions with museum colleagues whose specialty was Martian geology helped to round out their picture of Mars.

Photo of Mars

Computer-generated composite of Martian landscape

Model of Martian rock

Next Jacobs made a sketch showing how the exhibit might look. Over the months, as his understanding of Mars grew, he was able to add more and more detail. He portrayed a dry,

dusty, rocky terrain with rocks and soil that were a dull salmon pink.

To make the rocks, the museum hired a company that took molds from real rocks of the

American southwestern desert. These looked a lot like the rocks in the Viking Mars photographs. From these molds, the make-believe rocks were cast in a synthetic material, mounted on steel

Exhibit construction

Model builders at work

glow—much weaker than sunlight on Earth, because it is filtered through the dusty Martian atmosphere. He carefully hid the lightbulbs behind and among the rocks.

In the meantime, the museum hired an artist to create a painting that would provide a backdrop for the exhibit. Working under the same lighting conditions selected for the finished exhibit, the artist created a large painting on canvas. A team of museum experts then took color photographs of the painting in sections. Next they enlarged the photographs and pieced them together to make a mural approximately 6 meters (20 feet) high by 30 meters (100 feet) long, which they mounted on the wall.

Display panels, television monitors, mannequins in space suits, and robots were now added—and when they were finally finished, the exhibition team breathed a sigh of relief!

But wait—there was still one more thing to do. Everything looked too clean! Mars is, after all, an exceedingly *dusty* place. Space suits, robots, rocks, and other objects were painted to make them look slightly dusty.

frames, and airbrushed to produce a rocklike texture and color.

A planetary geologist from the museum brought in a soil sample from a volcano in Hawaii that had the same chemical composition as Martian soil. Using the Hawaiian soil as a model, the company was able to create make-believe soil for the exhibit.

The next challenge was creating the effect of Martian sunlight. The lighting designer experimented with different lightbulbs and their placement until he got the right pink

INTO THE UNKNOWN . . . AND BEYOND

"Where next?" is a very big question . . . and no one knows the answer for sure. As a member of the next generation, you'll play a role in deciding what happens. The answer in part is up to you!

But remember, when you search the night skies for comets or shooting stars—or chart the heavenly bodies in the museum's Planetarium—you join a long chain of explorers, discoverers, and stargazers. It began long before Columbus . . . and stretches as far into the future as your imagination can take you.

THIS PLACE IS HUGE!

Natural History, American History, Air and Space—they're just the tip of the iceberg when it comes to all the amazing things you can see and do at the Smithsonian. The following pages highlight a few special attractions you might want to discover in the Smithsonian's other thirteen museums and galleries, and the National Zoo.

In each museum, make the information desk your first stop. There you can get maps, tour schedules, and brochures about special exhibits. Many of the museums offer free activity books for kids, and this is the place to get them too.

FOR WASHINGTON KIDS

If you live in Washington, D.C., or plan to stay awhile, you'll want to check out the Smithsonian Associates. They sponsor lots of activities for kids and their families in the Washington area. Highlights include summer day camps, a yearly kite festival on the Mall, workshops and classes led by Smithsonian experts, and study tours. For information call (202) 357-3030.

The Smithsonian Associates also sponsor weekday and weekend performances for kids in the Discovery Theater, located in the Arts and Industries Building. For information call (202) 357-1500.

IF YOU CAN'T COME TO WASHINGTON

There are plenty of other ways to connect with the Smithsonian—even if you're not planning a visit to Washington, D.C. If

FUN

AT THE SMITHSONIAN

you have access to a computer with an on-line connection at home or at school, you may want to check out some of our resources electronically. It's an instant way of bringing the Smithsonian to you! Browsing our on-line resources is also a great way to catch up on what's current and see what's new at the "electronic" Smithsonian. For a Digital Directory, see p. 153.

TELL YOUR TEACHERS
The Smithsonian's Office of Elementary and Secondary Education offers current and back issues of the quarterly teaching guide *Art to Zoo*; the quarterly *Let's Go to the Smithsonian*, a guide for teachers visiting the Smithsonian; and lots more stuff for teachers to check out. For more information call (202) 357-2425.

THE OTHER THIRTEEN— A FEW BASICS

The Smithsonian museums on the following pages are open every day of the year, except December 25. Admission is free to all of the Smithsonian's Washington museums! Hours are 10:00 a.m. to 5:30 p.m., unless noted otherwise. Some of the Smithsonian museums

offer extended hours in the summer months. Call ahead for summer schedules so you can see and do more.

For the very latest information on all Smithsonian activities, please call Smithsonian Information at (202) 357-2700.

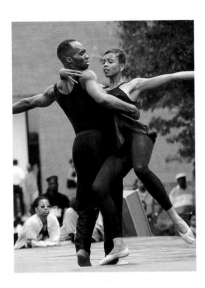

Anacostia Museum
1901 Fort Place, SE
(10:00 a.m. to 5:00 p.m.)
African American history and culture

Special African American history activities include exhibition tours, stories, art workshops, performances, and videos. The quarter-mile Dr. George Washington Carver Nature Trail—located next to the museum—lets you explore the natural environment and learn about the contributions of African American scientists. For more information, call (202) 287-3369.

Arthur M. Sackler Gallery
1050 Independence Avenue, SW
Asian art from ancient times to the present

The exhibition Puja: Expressions of Hindu Devotion features a recreation of a shrine in a Hindu temple. As you explore the museum, be on the lookout for sculptures of the Buddha, founder of the Buddhist religion. Free activity guides suggest ways to explore and discover more about many of the Sackler's exhibits. The "ImaginAsia" program also offers hands-on activities for kids accompanied by an adult. For more information, call (202) 357-3200.

Arts and Industries Building
Jefferson Drive SW next to the Smithsonian Castle
Philadelphia Centennial collections

"1876: A Centennial Exhibition" displays thousands of artifacts in the style of the great Philadelphia Centennial Exposition, from which many of the exhibits were acquired. Temporary exhibitions in the South Gallery offer a glimpse of African American history and life as a unique feature of American culture. In the magnificent, light-filled rotunda of the building, a fountain is surrounded by flowers and seasonal plants. Changing programs in the Discovery Theater include presentations by mimes, puppeteers, dancers, actors, and singers. For show times and reservations, call (202) 357-1500.

Freer Gallery of Art
Jefferson Drive at 12th Street, SW
Asian and late 19th- and early 20th-century American art

James McNeill Whistler's *Harmony in Blue and Gold: The Peacock Room* (shown above) will dazzle you with its gold, blue, and green peacocks and feathers covering the walls and ceiling. Pick up a free activity guide at the museum entrance to explore the room. Walk-in tours that include this room are offered daily. A seven-foot-tall wooden figure guards the entrance to an exhibition of Buddhist art. A "Superheroes" booklet, also available at the museum entrance, includes punch-out pieces you can use to create your own "superhero" statues like those in the museum. For more information, call (202) 357-3200.

Hirshhorn Museum and Sculpture Garden
Independence Avenue at
7th Street, SW
Modern painting and sculpture

The outdoor sculpture garden and plaza are filled with pieces such as Claes Oldenburg's *Geometric Mouse* and Kenneth Snelson's 65-foot-tall *Needle Tower*. (You'll want to reach out and touch these objects, but please don't.) Inside this donut-shaped museum, you'll especially enjoy Tony Craig's wall mosaic made of pieces of old toys and plastic objects, Joseph Cornell's boxes of mystery and imagination (who is that blue princess?), and Anselm Kiefer's massive painting with a huge metal book floating over a dark, barren landscape. Pick up a copy of the new Family Guide at the front desk. For more information, call (202) 357-3235.

National Museum of African Art
950 Independence Avenue, SW
Collection, study, and exhibition of African art

The exhibition Images of Power and Identity features a life-size figure (above) covered with hundreds of white, blue, and multi-colored beads from the kingdom of Bamum. The museum also offers films, musical performances, workshops, and storytelling of African folktales. For more information, call (202) 357-4600, ext. 221.

National Museum of American Art
8th and G Streets, NW
Painting, sculpture, graphics, folk art, and photography, 18th century to the present

A wonderful collection of folk art includes a five-foot-tall iron woman named *Marla,* a bottle-cap giraffe (above) and tiger, a quilt made from buttons, and a huge throne with furniture pieces all made from household objects covered with gold and silver foil. The museum also has an impressive collection of paintings of American Indians. Family days featuring music, dance, writing, and gallery activities are offered in conjunction with special exhibitions. For more information, call (202) 357-3095.

National Portrait Gallery
8th and F Streets, NW
Portraits of significant Americans

The Hall of Presidents includes portraits of every American president in paintings, sculpture, and photographs. The exhibition Champions of American Sport presents sports heroes you're sure to recognize. The portrait of Pocahontas by an unknown artist is a continual favorite. For more information, call (202) 357-2700.

National Postal Museum

2 Massachusetts Avenue at First
Street, NE

America's transportation and communication history and stamp collections

Check out the computer games that let you create original mail routes or "fly" an early airmail plane. Several short videos and animated films tell tales of the Pony Express and introduce "Owney," the world-famous postal dog. And don't forget to get your souvenir postcard metered and mailed—and see a computerized portrayal of the card's journey from Washington, D.C., to its destination. The Discovery Center is often open with special workshops and family events. For more information, call (202) 357-2991.

National Zoological Park

Entrances: Connecticut Avenue, NW (3000 block between Cathedral Avenue and Devonshire Place); Harvard Street and Adams Mill Road intersection; Beach Drive in Rock Creek Park

Check at the information booths for times of daily feedings of the panda, elephants, seals, sea lions, pelicans, and reptiles. Daily at 11:30 a.m., you can see elephant health care in the Elephant House or watch a seal and sea lion feeding and training demonstration. ZOOlab and HERPlab are two interactive learning centers that allow you to handle objects like elephant skins, bones and teeth, turtle shells and snake skins. And be

Winter hours:
Grounds: 8:00 a.m. to 6:00 p.m.
Buildings: 9:00 a.m. to 4:30 p.m.
Summer hours:
Grounds: 8:00 a.m. to 8:00 p.m.
Buildings: 9:00 a.m. to 6:00 p.m.
3,000 animals in a beautiful
163-acre park

sure to look *up*—the new "orangutan transport system" allows you to see orangutans traveling overhead on a series of cables between the Great Ape House and the fascinating new Think Tank exhibit. For more information, call (202) 673-4717 from 9 a.m. to 5 p.m. daily, or the 24-hour recording, (202) 673-4800.

Renwick Gallery of the National Museum of American Art

Pennsylvania Avenue at 17th
Street NW

American crafts

While you're sure to enjoy the American crafts on display here, it's also a great place to take a break. Sitting on a pouf—a comfy circular couch—in the enormous salon, you can gaze at nineteenth-century paintings stacked all the way up the walls. For more information, call (202) 357-2700.

IN NEW YORK CITY

DIGITAL DIRECTORY

National Museum of the American Indian, the George Gustav Heye Center

One Bowling Green, New York, NY
The Heye Center is located in the Alexander Hamilton U.S. Custom House, near Battery Park in lower Manhattan.
Native American objects from North, Central, and South America

After taking in the wonders of this museum's Native American artifacts, save some time to visit the Resource Center. Here you can learn more about the museum—as well as many aspects of native life and history—using the latest computer technology. For recorded information, call (212) 668-6624.

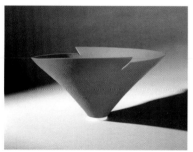

Cooper-Hewitt, National Design Museum

2 East 91st Street, New York, NY
Historical and contemporary design

The Carnegie Mansion, home of the National Design Museum, is exciting to explore. An activity guide about the Mansion's architecture and history is available in the Museum Shop. Family programs are offered throughout the year and include tours, workshops, demonstrations, and concerts. For more information, call (212) 860-6868.

INTERNET

(Address: *http://www.si.edu/*)
This reference directory for the Smithsonian Institution offers hypertext links to most other servers mentioned here.

WORLD WIDE WEB HOME PAGE:

A guide to the Smithsonian through its servers, organized by activities, people, perspectives, places, products, and resources. The Home Page has hypertext links to other electronic resources, including the following Smithsonian museums: Air and Space, American Art, American History, American Indian, Natural History. Some of these sites offer full-scale electronic exhibitions. Many offer visuals; you can also see and download pictures at the Smithsonian Institution Photo Server.
(Address: *ftp://photo1.si.edu*)

COMMERCIAL ON-LINE SERVICES

America Online/Smithsonian Online
(Keyword: *Smithsonian*)
Point-and-click format allows you to access up-to-date information on programs at many of the Smithsonian museums. View and download images. Check out Smithsonian books and recordings, or the latest from *Smithsonian* and *Air & Space* magazines. There's even a state-by-state listing of Smithsonian traveling exhibitions that may be coming your way. For more information on America Online/Smithsonian Online, call (800) 827-6364, extension 7822.

The Smithsonian also has photographic material for viewing and downloading on Compuserve (800) 848-8199 and Genie (800) 638-9636.

IF YOUR TEACHER'S WIRED

The Smithsonian's Office of Elementary and Secondary Education offers materials for teachers online via the Internet (Address: *ftp to educate.si.edu*) Teaching-related materials can also be accessed through America Online/Smithsonian Online.

KIDS' TOP 40

We'd love to hear what you think! Send your list of Smithsonian favorites to: Kids' Top 40, Book Development Division, Smithsonian Institution Press, 470 L'Enfant Plaza, Suite 7100, Washington, DC 20560

The author would like to thank: Wendy Aibel-Weiss, David Allison, Bob Beauchamp, Michael Brett-Surman, Leni Buff, Teresia Bush, Spencer Crew, Doug Casey, Dorothy Dunn, James Early, Nate Erwin, Barney Finn, Jacqueline Grazette, Robert Hall, Charlotte Heth, Robert Hoffman, Dave Jenkins, Laura Kennedy, Karen Lee, Ed Lifschitz, Tom Lowderbaugh, Nancy McCoy, Laura McKie, Valerie Neal, Beth Norden, Larry O'Reilly, Heather Paisley-Jones, Nora Panzer, Lucia Pierce, Jeff Post, Sarita Rodriguez, Ray Rye, Michelle Smith, Steven Soter, Christopher Stetser, Bob Sullivan, Doug Ubelaker, Roger White, Bill Withuhn, and Sarah Wiley.

The Smithsonian Press staff would like to thank Barbara Embury Hehner, Rubber Chicken Enterprises, Blue Heron, our expert advisors Christina Dahlman and Alexandra Goodwin, Jim Anthony, Frances Rowsell, Linda's dog (for not eating pictures), and colleagues at the Smithsonian who helped with this book.

Special thanks to the Office of Printing and Photographic Services, and to Mark Avino, David Burgevin, Chip Clark, Jessie Cohen, Harold Dorwin, Carl Hansen, Franko Khoury, Eric Long, Laurie Minor-Penland, Dane Penland, Jeff Ploskonka, Richard Strauss, Jeff Tinsley, and Jim Wallace.